Also by Robert Brancatelli

The Gringo
Laura Fedora

Nine Lives

Robert Brancatelli

Blumen Publishing

New York

For Edgar, Arthur, and Ryder.

"The main difference between a cat and a lie is that a cat only has nine lives."

Mark Twain
The Tragedy of Pudd'nhead Wilson

Introduction

They say that cats have nine lives. Although my landlord won't let me have a cat, I have observed them over the years and have come to the conclusion that this is true. If not in a literal sense, it is certainly true metaphorically, which, after all, is more important. Like cats, people also have nine lives. Most choose not to live all of them, and it is a sad fact that some people do not even live one. They simply go about their business without noticing or doing much of anything. But that is their choice. You can play ball or sit in the stands and watch. It's up to you. It all depends on what you want and where you want to go. And if you don't care where you go, "then it doesn't matter at all," as the Cheshire Cat said to Alice.

I care where I go, even if at times it has seemed otherwise. Like a cat, I have meandered, wandered, and slunk down blind alleys only to scale back up concrete walls onto a fire escape into the sunlight again. All right, that is a bit of an exaggeration, since most of my slinking has occurred at night, but the rest is true, living, as I do, in a land of fire escapes. Over the years, I have not done anything other than remain true to my cat nature, which is to meander, wander, and slink. Occasionally I strut, but most of the time I maintain a sophisticated gait. It is all so deceiving, because in reality I have no idea where I am going. Don't let a pair of green eyes fool you. But then most people don't know where they are going, not even those neurotic types who plan, measure, and map out with GPS accuracy the trajectory of their lives. It is all so neat and controlled until one day a baby floats by in a bulrush basket daubed with pitch and your life is never the same (got that from Milan Kundera). Neither is history, since the baby is Moses and you bend down and scoop him into your arms. There is freedom in the bending and scooping, freedom that you would not have had if you had ignored the basket and continued bathing, concerned with nothing more than slipping on rocks.

Thanks to Robert Frost, we know that way leads on to way and that once you start down one path, it is pretty near impossible to turn around and take another. But whereas paths in the woods vary, the lives of cats do not. That is, their nine lives may be distinct and separate, but they are not so different that you couldn't identify a certain theme, thread, or musical phrase running through each one of them. The theme depends on the particular cat, but, once you find it, you have the key to understanding everything else about that cat: what it likes to eat, where it rests from the midday sun, how it fares with the other cats in the neighborhood.

The same is true of you and me. You can't run away from who you are. So, even if two roads diverged in a yellow wood, it might not matter which one you took, because *you* are the one taking it. The free will with which you act is *yours,* which means that the one constant in every possible scenario (e.g., the high road, the low road, the bog, the job in Kansas City, the dancer in Paris) is *you*. And, as anyone older than twelve has discovered, you can't escape you. Aristotle went further than that, declaring that "nobody would choose to have all the good things in the world at the price of becoming somebody else" (*Nicomachean Ethics*). So, even when they figure out how to move your consciousness from neurons to fiber optic cables as in the Star Trek episode, "Spock's Brain," it will still be *your* consciousness, soul, brain in the computer. There's no getting around it this side of death. Buddhists and Christians disagree about the other side of death, of course, but as long as you're still breathing, you have to work with what you've got, even if it takes nine times to get it right.

It has taken me more than nine times to get this life right, and I still don't have it down. How is it that I am still here? There are a couple of possibilities: I am living on borrowed time, I miscalculated the number of lives I have used thus far, I am about to die. I'm not crazy about any of these, especially the last one, but you have to remember that we're dealing with metaphor here. "Nine lives" is a metaphor. Of what, exactly? I could answer by waxing poetic, but I'll spare you. I'll simply say it is a metaphor of various states and abilities. By states, I mean that none of us is one thing and one thing only. We have many facets and dimensions, each one holding the potential for a different kind of existence, an alternate you, except it isn't an alternate you. It's the real you even as you drift in and out of parallel universes.

Chuck Schumer, the senator from my home state of New York, likes to tell the story of how he was faced with a dilemma upon graduation from college years ago. He could either accept a prestigious award, which included a one-year, paid trip around the world, or decline the award to stay home and marry the girl of his dreams. Romantic that he is, he picked the girl, who thereupon dumped him a few months later. So, he ended up losing both the trip and the girl. I know the senator likes to tell this story, because he told it at commencement at Fordham University. It's also on YouTube. It reminded me of the sixties' gameshow, "Let's Make A Deal," and how Monty Hall would give contestants the choice of Door Number One, Two, or Three. Sometimes they'd get lucky and pick the door that had a shiny, red convertible behind it. Other times, they'd end up with a year supply of dog food. They say that if given a choice between keeping your original door and switching, your odds double by switching. Two-thirds are better than one-half; something like that. Still, you never know.

By abilities, I mean that most of us have more than one trick up our sleeve. We can be good at solving quadratic equations, playing the flute, writing haiku, designing kitchens, or hacking into government Web sites. I'm not saying you should feel inferior if you aren't good at half a dozen things, just that most people have varied interests and skills. I'm not sure how that works with genius, however. Malcolm Gladwell believes you have to concentrate on one thing for about ten years before you master it. That could be true, but does that mean to the exclusion of everything else? If so, it would explain why I wouldn't want Mozart doing my taxes or Alan Turing giving me fashion advice. My point is that each one of these interests could lead to an entirely different life or lives, all within your lifetime. For instance, I have developed a sudden interest in opera (seriously). If it were to develop into something, I could conceivably end up on stage dressed like the father of the step-sisters in Rossini's *Cinderella*. Hey, it could happen. I never thought I'd be in Brazil giving a business seminar in Portuguese, but that's exactly what happened. *Nunca se sabe.*

The following vignettes are arranged in somewhat chronological order from my college years through marriage, family, work, and parenting. Like the nine lives of a cat, there is a thread running through them, which I have pointed out from time to time, hopefully without hitting the reader over the head. That is a principle I try to follow as a writer: not hitting the reader over the head. It doesn't help sales. The thread is simple. It is *grace*. By grace, I do not mean the relationship between will and grace as in the writings of one of my favorite philosophers, Martin Buber, or the popular sitcom with that redhead and gay guy, but grace as in the hand of God reaching down to save me from my own stupidity. If that had not happened—had God continued wading in the water and ignored me in the basket—I would not have survived to write about that brazen stupidity. And you would not be reading it.

You may find some of these stories insensitive, perhaps offensive. I apologize in advance. I am not so skilled a writer that I know how to present the bizarre realities of life in any other way. Often, I get caught up in the details without seeing the forest, as it were. "Angelina in a Casket" is a good example. There, I make fun not only of a dead relative but of a psychologically disabled veteran. Elsewhere, I lampoon friends, colleagues, and family members. Think of it as a variation of friends, Romans, and countrymen. "But Can You Type," "Misery, the Mother of Intention," and "These Boots Are Made for Walkin" are good examples of these. For the most part, names have been changed to protect the innocent and avoid litigation from those with thin skin and thick wallets. Sadly, we live in an age when lawyers abound and justice is hard to find. So sometimes you have to lie to tell the truth, which is what I have done. Everything in these stories is a fabrication, sort of like Levittown, but then again all truth is based on lies. Or is it the other way around? I am reminded of Peter Sellers playing Inspector Clouseau when he declares that he suspects everyone and he suspects no one. Then he rubs cold cream on his nose.

In the stories that follow, whether involving the tall, the sad, the glad, or the myriad kinds of people in between, I have found God's grace at work everywhere and in everyone. This is true even with the person I make the most fun of: *moi*. In the background, I can also hear the voice of Gerard Manley Hopkins. In his poem, "As Kingfishers Catch Fire" (1918), he writes in a similar way, finding Christ

> in ten thousand places, /
> Lovely in limbs,
> and lovely in eyes not his /
> To the father through the features

of men's faces. (lines 12-14)

Finally, I would like to thank Joan Cavanagh of Fordham University for her wise counsel as my spiritual director in working through the Spiritual Exercises of St. Ignatius. It isn't easy tearing yourself apart and stitching yourself back together again on a regular basis. Having a co-conspirator is essential. Joan also helped me identify the theme of grace. I have taken it up elsewhere (i.e., The Brancatelli Blog), because of its consistent presence in my life and the lives of so many others I have been fortunate enough to know.

R. Brancatelli
New York City
August 15, 2015
Feast of The Assumption

Angelina in a Casket

You could say that my childhood was just like everybody else's, but you'd be wrong. Sure, all the outward signs were there. We had a nice house on Staten Island, two cars (one a big, white Cadillac convertible with a red-leather interior and power windows), an above-ground pool with a lot of chlorine, pets, FWB (Friends with Braces), grandparents, and a respectable amount of money to throw around on everything from baseball cleats to California vacations. We even looked the part. When my parents married in 1955, my father was twenty-two and my mother nineteen. He was just out of the Air Force with wavy, red hair and ready to start a family. My mother was model material, all legs (they called her "a long drink of water"), and worked as a secretary in downtown Manhattan for IBM. Not bad at all. We four kids blended seamlessly into the neighborhood, too, which was made up almost entirely of Jews and Italians. Most of the time you couldn't tell the difference between the two, except the Jewish kids didn't wear gold necklaces with crosses and had bat and bar mitzvahs, which, to be honest, we were a little envious of. Christmas made up for it, though. Jews didn't celebrate it then the way they do now. Today, everybody celebrates Christmas: Hindus, Buddhists, atheists, Korean store owners, even Jehovah's Witnesses. It's almost not worth the effort anymore. Macy's has coopted the holiday.

As normal as my family looked on the outside, however, we were anything but on the inside. It was like those rock and roll documentaries when they say, "But backstage the band was falling apart." We weren't falling apart; we just didn't conform to the image other people had of us. I know this, because people were always surprised when they discovered that my grandmother cared for mentally disabled teens, or that my Uncle Enrico had paranoid schizophrenia and thought the Japanese were bombing us, or that my grandfather was married to another woman before he met my grandmother, or that my mother's Aunt Josie had a weakness for Manhattans and young male companionship. I can assure you that there was nothing sinister or immoral about us. Well, unless you're one of those holier than thou people who consider abandoning dogs in the woods and stealing Christmas ornaments from the local drug store immoral. We were just a little different.

Angelina was my grandfather's sister. We didn't know much about her beyond her name and the fact that she was older than my grandfather, which was hard enough to comprehend, considering that my grandfather was in the army in World War I. I asked my grandmother once which army, but she set me straight right away and said the American one, what was I a wiseguy? I wasn't a wiseguy, not in the cable television sense, but I certainly was a wiseass (aka know-it-all, wisenheimer, smart aleck—cue The Marvelettes of *Smart Aleck* and *Beechwood 4-5789* fame). Being a wiseass has gotten me into so much trouble over the years that I wonder how I have survived. Then again, there really wasn't any other way to get by in my house. You had to be quick on your feet, literally and metaphorically, and have skin as thick as a manatee, which none of us had. Apparently, we must have all been artists, because we had artistic temperaments. There just wasn't any artwork to show for it, at least not right away. My brother turned out to be a talented artist even though he doesn't like to show his work to anybody, which I find more than a little ironic. What do you do with a bashful painter? (That's not rhetorical; I'm really asking). I advised him to cut his ear off and post pictures of it on Facebook, but he wouldn't hear of it.

Getting back to my grandfather, I thought it was a perfectly reasonable question about which army, since I had never heard him speak English except for "hammel," which was his way of saying "hammer," and "two eggs," which was what he ate every morning for breakfast. Turns out the war ended while he was headed to England on a troop transport. So, technically, he was in the army but not the war, which is probably the best way to do it. Besides, you can't be in a war if you're on your way to it. Being late for a war just might be a new moral statement.

Then one day Angelina died. My father came home to announce that his favorite aunt had just passed away from old age. It didn't seem possible that anyone could die from being old, but I accepted it just as I accepted that this was his "favorite" aunt. I had never heard him talk about anyone in his family except to say disparaging things about them and that he never wanted to see any of them again. You'd think that would be hard to do, what with my grandfather having five brothers and sisters, each of whom went on to have families of their own and all of them living no farther than Brooklyn to the east and Red Bank to the west. The amazing thing was that we never saw or ran into any of them, so I guess it was more than possible. That reminds me of the time years later when Rose, my daughter, ran into my Uncle Frankie at a circus in Las Vegas of all places. He had been sitting behind her in the stands and leaned over to get a better look.

"I thought she looked familiar," he told me later.

Whenever I tell people that story they look at me in shock, since Italians have a reputation for warmth, generosity, and big families with women with even bigger breasts. People assume there's a table overflowing with food and music playing in the background in every Italian household. Well, not my household. We're closer to the cable television variety of Italians, but nobody ever talks about that, except maybe in the coffee shops on Arthur Avenue in the Bronx. Make sure you sit facing the door.

Aunt Angelina was dead, that was a fact. Another fact was that my father was worried about how my grandfather would take the news, what with them being so close. Angelina had reared my grandfather in a tenement on East 108th Street in Manhattan, which was where a lot of Italians went when they came to this country, especially ones from the Molise-Abruzzo region of Italy. The interesting thing is that my great grandfather, Francescoantonio, came in 1887 before the opening of Ellis Island. His wife and half of the children came later; the other half, including my grandfather, were born here, which explains his being a Doughboy. All eight of them and a family friend were listed in the 1900 US census, which I have copies of. I know these things, because I am the family historian and have spent many hours hunched over a hot microfiche at the National Archives. It's just what I do.

"I think we should tell him in a letter," my father said after serious reflection.

"A letter?" my mother repeated.

"That's right, a letter. He'll read it and then he can react in his own way. That way, nobody has to bring him the bad news."

All of a sudden there was this dread of delivering bad news, which I didn't get at all. It was as if we were living in the time of ancient biblical kings when whoever brought bad news was impaled against the wall with a spear.

"So, who writes the letter?" my mother, always the practical one, asked.

"I don't know. We'll have a contest, I guess."

"A contest?"

"Sure, why not? We'll all write something and the best one wins."

"How do we know which one is the best?"

"We'll just know," my father said, getting irritated.

"Do we write it in English?" I asked.

"Don't be a wiseass," my mother said.

So we sat around the kitchen table like Knights of the Round Table to write our letters. To tell you the truth, it was a lot harder than I thought. First off, I wasn't sure if this was a business letter, a friendly letter, a persuasive letter, or like something you'd get from the dentist. I hated birthday cards from the dentist, but no matter how many times I'd mention it in passing as we had our teeth cleaned, I still got them like clockwork. So, I ruled that out. It also couldn't be a business letter, what with this being my grandfather and we didn't have a business relationship. Actually, we didn't have any relationship other than him threatening us with the belt. So I had to come up with some other format.

Now, there's an advantage to having a college education, and it is perhaps most evident at times like these. As Joey Balducci in my Public Speaking class at Ursinus College in Collegeville, Pennsylvania once observed, "A college education allows you to bullshit on any subject anywhere at any time." He then proceeded to bullshit the class on some topic related to screen passes (he was on the football team, no surprise there), which had nothing at all to do with a college education. Nevertheless, we all know that a college education broadens your mind, sharpens your critical thinking skills, and gets you laid (on-campus students mostly). It also justifies rebelling against your parents and questioning everything anybody ever said to you. All you have to do is accuse something of being "anecdotal" and the game is over. The opposing party hasn't got a leg to stand on. See, anecdotal can't be any good, because it's just somebody's very unscientific analysis of a very vague phenomenon by a very imperceptible and flawed mind. In other words, anything unscientific and experiential couldn't possibly be any good, because there's no hard data to support it, and God help you if you bring up intuition or mystery. You'll be treated with contempt and disdain as an old school sentimentalist, probably somebody who eats butterscotch pudding. "Anecdotal" works like a trump or a Get-Out-of-Jail card. The minute anybody throws it down, they win. If you happen to wear a lab coat or have gone to the University of Chicago, even better. And, please, don't get me started about cultural Marxism and the most intolerant place on earth: American universities.

At the time, I was the only person in our family in college. In fact, I was the first person in our family on either side to go to college. That, combined with the fact that I was the first-born male, meant that I was just below Jesus Christ in the pecking order. Anything higher than me would have required a miracle like walking on water or resurrecting the dead. But—and this is important—I was destined for greatness not because of anything I thought or said or did, but because of fate. Fate, *fato*, is extremely important for Italians. It is related to *fatalità*, which is related to *calamità*, which, in turn, is related to *morte* or death. It also has to do with fortune (*fortuna*) and misfortune (*sfortuna*). You might be fated one way or another, but once the die is cast (*alea iacta est*), the only thing you can do is accept your fate or reject it and risk an end like Actaeon, who was turned into a stag by the goddess Diana and then torn apart by his own hunting hounds. Rather dramatic if you ask me, but that's the ancient world for you. It continues to influence how Italians and Italian Americans view life, death, God, and the cosmos.

In case you didn't catch it, all of this is the long way of saying that, because of my college education, I knew what haiku was but nobody else did, which gave me what some might consider an unfair advantage. Another thing about our family (I'm not sure if this was due to our cultural heritage or just our particular way of doing things), is that there was no such thing as an "unfair" advantage. You either had an advantage or you didn't. If you made it fair, then it wouldn't be an advantage at all, thus undermining the very thing that was going to help you come out on top. What was the point of having an advantage if you were going to share it with somebody else? It didn't make any sense, which brings to mind the near violent argument at dinner one night about the Reagan Administration's offer to share our Star Wars technology with the Russians. My father was adamantly against it ("What in God's name were they thinking?") and went on a tirade about how Americans didn't understand how the real world worked and were too pampered. For instance, Truman didn't get how vicious the Red Chinese were and so he let them off the hook, which was a huge mistake.

"He should have given them a left hook, not off the hook!" my father said.

Like an unfair advantage, kicking someone when he's down was not only understood in my house but admired as an act of bravado and undeniable proof that you had "hair on your chest." Oddly enough, haiku had the potential to put hair on my chest, so I wasn't about to share it with the rest of the family, even though all they had come up with for the contest were ridiculously formal letters that said things like, "It is with great regret that I inform you..." It was as if we were corresponding with widows for the War Department. After three hours, all we had to show for our efforts were a growing pile of crumpled loose leaf paper, bored looks, and empty espresso cups. I took a shot at haiku, forgot the rhyme structure, went to my bedroom to consult my poetry book (three lines, seventeen syllables max), and came back refreshed for another round. By then, we had taken to reading the drafts, each person standing up and reciting what they had written, receiving either applause or booing when finished. My younger brother had become an expert at the armpit fart and chose to regale us with his artistry whenever he saw fit, which was pretty much after each reading.

We spent two more hours trying our hand at various forms of corporate communication such as interoffice letters, memoranda of understanding, and the opening paragraph of the actual death certificate. Nothing worked. Then, out of desperation, we took a stab at poetry, and it occurred to me that that is probably how most poetry is written, which means it's found rather than created. Kind of like stepping in a puddle that's deeper than you thought or finding out that the woman you've been dating is an ex-con. Our family loved the "roses are red" genre, which is one rung below the literary quality of greeting cards. My sister, Jolie, college-bound and sassy, stood up and recited the following:

> Roses are red,
> violets are blue.
> So is Angelina
> from her head
> to her shoe.

Nicely done, with good pacing and rhythm, I thought. She received warm applause, to which she curtsied, and a short, high-pitched fart from my brother. It was like a foghorn in the stands at graduation.

"I guess that means Aunt Angelina will have to wear blue shoes in the casket," I said. "Or maybe just one blue shoe."

"Is that so? Well, what about you, college boy?" my father retaliated. "All that money and we can't even get a letter out of you. What are they teaching you in that fancy school of yours?"

There was an edge in his voice that I recognized as coming not just from blue shoes but our ongoing competition to be the alpha male, which had gotten worse since my fifteenth birthday. The day I turned fifteen, he came home with a birthday cake that he had gotten for half-price at La Rosa's, because it said "Happy Birthday, Richard." Apparently, Richard's parents never picked it up. Truthfully, though, we had gotten off to a bad start when, as a baby, I would bite the rubber nipples off my bottles and hurl the bottles of warm formula at him grenade style from my crib as he sat studying for the Fire Department entrance exam.

"I'm working on it," I said.

"Working on what?"

"It's a special kind of poem."

"What's so special about it?"

"It's called haiku."

Silence.

"Isn't that aftershave?"

"No, it's Japanese."

Big mistake, that. It brought up World War Two, Hiroshima (to drop or not to drop), transistor radios, and Datsuns, not to mention my brother reenacting the bombing of Pearl Harbor with his armpit.

"I need more time," I said.

"You've got twenty minutes before dinner," my mother said. She had already begun clearing the table of pens and paper, making room for the dishes.

Twenty minutes isn't a long time, but inspiration can happen in an instant. It can be triggered by little things. Jolie's line about Angelina being blue from her head to her shoe got me thinking about the time, just a month prior, when we had to inform my uncle that his aunt had died (not sure why, but aunts were dropping like flies at the time). My parents decided to let my grandfather tell him, warning him that Uncle Enrico, who was heavily-medicated on antipsychotic drugs, was very fragile and any sudden shock could do even more damage. They had also given my grandfather my uncle's hat to return to him, which he had left during his last visit home. As soon as they pulled up to the hospital, my grandfather, who was not exactly what you would call spry, jumped out of the car, handed my uncle his hat and said, "Here's your hat, Rae died!" He claimed later that he had only wanted to soften the blow, but it took my uncle months to recover. Now, as I saw it, both Jolie's and my grandfather's messages had something in common. They were direct, clear, and made use of concrete symbols to get their point across: a shoe and a hat. I needed to do the same thing. But how?

Now, here's the thing. When I say that my childhood wasn't like everybody else's, I don't mean we had it better or worse or were richer or poorer than other people, or even that we were a little eccentric in some way compared to what was normal. I mean we lived according to a completely different standard. We weren't one thing or another relative to our neighbors; we weren't in any kind of relation to them. Think of an Italian-American Addams Family and then add episodes that include torching a moving truck for insurance money, stealing a Christmas tree from Borough Hall, and playing softball with developmentally disabled kids at a state mental facility (i.e., Willowbrook). I realize that these might reinforce a certain stereotype of Italians that is all but extinct. My kids wouldn't even recognize it, but I am old enough to remember being called a wop and ginny as well as the look of surprise on a classmate's face when she noted how clean I was "for an Italian." That was in Southern New Jersey, which is another story. My apologies, too, to Mario Cuomo, who pointed out on numerous occasions that not all Italian-Americans are mobsters and not all mobsters say "bada-bing." Chris Christie may be another matter. The point here is that the things that made my family different were not a function of our being Italian, Italian-American, or New Yorkers but were unique to our family.

I have thought long and hard about this over the years, because it is important to know the source of your suffering. It isn't enough to say, "Well, it's me and my tendency to sabotage myself," or, "If I had just gotten into that graduate school, things would be different now." Seriously, what's that got to do with anything? You'd be the same after grad school except another hundred grand in debt. So, when I say I know the source of my suffering, our suffering, I am not saying it lightly. Neither have I taken the easy way out and blamed other people. Well, I am blaming other people, but only because it's true. See, I don't know if it's a curse or because of some misaligned star somebody in the family was born under five hundred years ago in the cold hills of Provvidenti, our ancestral town, but our peculiarity is the direct result of—now get this—*women*. That probably sounds funny or bizarre or sexist, but I don't mean it to be. Neither do I mean just any women. I mean the mothers in our family.

"Wait a minute," you may say. "Don't a lot of women become mothers? How many nuns have you produced?"

Actually, I can't be sure. I am guessing none (!), but the short answer is no, they don't all qualify as mothers, not the kind I have in mind. There are women in the family who get married, have kids, and lead normal lives, sure, but then there are those who emit such a powerful magnetic force that it's as if the psychic energy of our entire genealogical tree gets sucked into them like water circling a drain, or a black hole. If there are supernovas, these women are "super mothers" who exist in a different category entirely.

Now, before you storm off into the backyard or garden to scream at the apparent souring of what up till now had been a promising short story about a woman named Angelina and a casket, let me explain. Even given the dramatic nature of these super moms, there is still only one condition under which there is an implosion of such magnitude that it is like matter and anti-matter coming into contact with each other. That condition is when two super moms are in a mother/daughter-in-law relationship. One is matter (Mother Matter) and the other anti-matter (Daughter-Anti-Law). If such a condition exists, then the resulting melt-down of the genetic structure and vaporization of the family tree leads to the phenomenon I described at the beginning of this story. What appears as normal on the outside is anything but on the inside. Let the record show that this is an irrefutable and immutable fact. There's no undoing what has been done by the fundamental forces of nature. I have no idea how God fits into this and wouldn't presume to know about free will except to say that the energy released in this collision compares to what occurs on the surface of the sun. Only a lot worse.

The situation in our family is a case in point. My mother and grandmother conducted what can only be described as a Hundred Years War and, even though it did not last that long, it seemed as if it did, wreaking as much havoc as if it had lasted not one but two hundred years. In fact—and this is a result of the matter/anti-matter collision—it will take generations before the family is able to regain the stability it had prior to contact. Radioactive isotopes are buzzing around the garage like mosquitos and you'd better take a Geiger Counter into the bathroom with you when you visit. To make matters worse, there is yet another phenomenon ("singularity" physicists call it) in which this relationship of matter and anti-matter is repeated in successive generations so that you can have a chain in which a Mother Matter collides with a Daughter-Anti-Law, who, in turn, acts as Mother Matter to a second Daughter-Anti-Law. Imagine billiard balls smacking into each other all over the pool table. Such is my case and the real reason for this book. To put it as simply as I can, my grandmother's relationship to my mother was replicated in my mother's relationship to my wife. I'd say it again, but it's too painful. You'll just have to reread the sentence. If all of this is confusing to you, imagine what it was like for me. This is the reason I had a midlife crisis that lasted from the age of twenty-three to fifty-four. Well, one of the reasons.

To figure out how all of this started or who is responsible would be pointless, since you'd need an entire forensics team from one of those television shows, an FBI profiler, and the Psychology Department at a major university to get anywhere. It's probably not worth it, since what has been done cannot be undone, as noted earlier, although it would be nice to dig a fire line in the ground to prevent further damage. That's mixing metaphors, but everything is mixed up now, anyway, with me and my siblings carrying both sides in us: my grandmother and my mother. So, we may be walking time bombs, especially when you consider that my mother's family is Sicilian, which means hotheaded and vengeful with wit as sharp as a steel edge. My grandfather didn't even consider Sicilians Italian, which aggravated my mother no end. That sentiment spilled over into the neighborhood from time to time, even during the late 60s and early 70s, when I was called a half-breed for being only "half Italian."

"Time's up, what have you got?" my father demanded.

The rest of them sat around the table, looking up at me. Mom was at the kitchen sink, pretending not to hear anything but overhearing everything.

"Okay, here it is," I said.

I cleared my throat, adjusted the paper a couple of times, and cleared my throat again.

"For chrissakes, get on with it!"

"Right."

I had come up with something pretty clever, I thought, not for any brilliance of its own, but because of its simplicity, which is the whole point of haiku. You don't waste words or images or ideas. It's pretty spare and disciplined, which is what you would expect from a people who invented samurai swords. Of course, they also had calligraphy and plum wine, and that's why balance is so important in haiku. You balance opposites like darkness and light, and in the contrast you find truth. Something like that. Anyway, I had discovered the image I had been looking for ever since hearing Jolie's poem. What I needed was something to represent death, and what's a very concrete symbol for death?

"Can I have a glass of water?" I asked.

There was a collective moan, my father mumbled, "unbelievable," and my brother launched a rapid-fire attack of armpit farts. Mom, shaking her head, handed me a glass of water and stood over me, waiting.

"Read it," she said with Sicilian finality.

You don't mess with that, believe me. I finished the water and, holding the paper up to my face so as not to look at them directly, recited the following:

> In a tree,
> in a basket.
> Angelina in a casket.

There was a moment of silence during which blood rushed to my ears, but this was followed by a cascade of applause. My mother placed her hand on my shoulder, nearly in tears, and my brother issued celebratory farts like they were going out of style. My entry won Best Death Poem by acclamation (we're nothing if not democratic), and everyone felt relieved that the contest had finally ended. Even my father swallowed his competitive pride, looked me square in the eye, and congratulated me with a firm handshake, man-to-man.

Afterward, we ate dinner in silence, which was rare, and then went our separate ways. We never spoke of it again. Nor did we give my grandfather the poem. My father told him about Angelina in the car ride to the funeral parlor, all of us dressed in black, which, strangely enough, never tipped him off. It was probably better that way. The haiku would have confused him. He wasn't the kind of guy given to poetry or sentiment. He had worked for the Department of Sanitation for years during a time when they still used horse-drawn wagons. Shit had been abundant in his life; he didn't need any more of it. But the exercise served a greater purpose, as I look back on it now.

Some families play cribbage, others play card games like gin rummy and poker. We wrote funerary haiku. It was just one of the things we did. That alone didn't make us peculiar. I mean, it could have been worse. We could have collected entrails in clay jars or flooded the basement to reenact naval battles. What made us peculiar was the fact that we thought nothing of it, enjoyed it no end, and knew that it would make no difference whatsoever how my grandfather found out. Now, that's how you make memories.

"But Can You Type?"

When I first moved to California from Center City, Philadelphia, where I had been living after college, I auditioned for a job delivering singing telegrams. In the audition, I had to wear a gorilla suit, since the message service offered a variety of getups that people could choose from to get their point across, gorillas being one of them. The message I was delivering was from a girl to a guy to let him know that she thought he was a big ape and could sit on an unripe banana for all she cared. It ended with a big finish on one knee and my arms spread out like Al Jolson singing *Mammy*, which, if you've never tried before, is hard to do in a gorilla suit. I got the job, but it wasn't long before I realized that it wasn't for me. First off, it was humiliating having to wear costumes to offices, hair salons, and restaurants. Second, although I have a decent enough voice that has gotten me into church choirs (I've even been a third-string organist), I didn't have the kind of Broadway, hit-people-in-the-back-row voice that got the biggest tips. Third, and most important of all, it had the potential to be dangerous. I mean, singing to a guy in a gorilla suit that he is a big ape and can sit on a banana in front of his buddies or boss can land you on your pink gorilla behind in no time. I don't know if they actually have pink behinds, but you catch my meaning. What I learned from the job, though, which was an invaluable lesson, was that some jobs were not right for me. Singing telegrams was one of them. It might have worked for my friend, George, who during college had a job where he dressed up like a Twinkie at the local

Kroger's, but it wasn't my cup of tea. The other thing I learned was that the opposite must be true; that is, there had to be a job out there with my name on it. Finding it was the real challenge.

I should explain what I mean. See, for me finding a job has never been a problem. I've had all kinds of jobs, from singing in the gorilla suit to selling ice cream, cars, advertising space, insurance, and real estate limited partnerships (not all at the same time, mind you). The problem is finding the right job in the right place at the right time for the right reasons, which is a purely Aristotelian approach. It's true that if you're unhappy, even though you make six figures, you'll make everyone around you unhappy, too. It's not worth the money. The trick is finding a job that you love and pays well. I don't have that formula down just yet. Most of the time, I end up with jobs that I love but do not pay well, or jobs that I detest that do not pay well. There's another variant of that formula I need to work on. So far, though, I haven't had much luck. In order to find the job that's right for you, you have to know who you are and what you want. Remember the Cheshire Cat? You might be able to do a hundred things, but what's the one thing you really want to do and why? Potential employers, if they're any good, will know before you do. Like that August afternoon right out of college when I sat for hours waiting to be interviewed by a jewelry guy who herded a bunch of us dazed graduates into a backroom, gave a perfunctory spiel about his product—cubic zirconium—and then demanded to know if we had what it took to make it in the cubic zirconium business (I thought it was an element and sat there trying to figure out is symbol on the Periodic Table). The index cards we had filled out were in alphabetical order, so my name was first, naturally. Where's a kid named Johnny Anderson when you need him?

"Well?" the jewelry guy asked, fumbling my name.

"Well, what?"

"Do you have what it takes?"

"I-I-I dunno," I stuttered.

"If you don't know, then we don't want you, good-bye," he said coldly, moving on to the next terrified victim.

"But—"

"Good-bye...Cynthia Burns!"

This happened in Manhattan's Diamond District, so, drenched with sweat and humiliation, I hobbled over to the Hebrew Studies section of the New York Public Library, which was air conditioned (not all buildings were in 1978). I sat down very quietly and cried. Whimpered, really. Then I ate my warm bologna sandwich that I had packed in the Samsonite briefcase Aunt Frances had given me for graduation. I was wearing a gray, three-piece woolen suit (my only one) and pouring sweat like a prizefighter. It had a pullover sweater instead of a button-down vest and would have been a sharp-looking outfit for February. I had tried to make it look like the most natural thing in the world. I suppose anything short of passing out was a success. The scene was so pathetic even the guard looked the other way. I didn't know it at the time, but I was in good company. There is a story concerning John D. Rockefeller, Sr. doing the same thing in Cleveland at the age of sixteen when he was looking for a way to escape his crazy family. He spent six weeks walking up and down the "Flats" everyday looking for work. He wore a dark suit, high collar, and black tie. "The streets were so hot and hard that he grew footsore from pacing them."[1] Of course he did. It's more painful that way.

---

[1] I didn't intend this to be an academic paper with footnotes, but I have to include them from time to time. I hope the reader understands. It's an occupational hazard. So, here's the reference to an excellent book: Ron Chernow, *Titan: The Life of John D. Rockefeller, Sr.* (New York: Vintage Books, 1998), 44-46.

In addition to knowing who you are, you have to be able to say no. That's a huge lesson in life and takes a lot of practice. A lot of failure, too. We are accustomed to saying yes all the time and want to please others, but that's not a formula for success. For instance, I should have told the jewelry guy no right up front and saved myself a lot of aggravation. But I didn't know how. If you can't say no, then you're setting yourself up for every shoeshine and smile that comes along, as Arthur Miller might say. But I don't want to do that. I want to get things right. How do you get things right? I'm still figuring that out, but I know most people get things wrong. We can even spend years living under a false notion of reality, which is what I did. What I am afraid of is that I have passed this inability down to my children.

Take this editing job I had once in Monterey, California (please). I knew the instant I set foot onto the premises that it wasn't the job for me. It even *smelled* wrong. Seriously, I could smell the dysfunction as if it were ejecting spores from the air vents. All right, maybe that's an exaggeration, but not much. My suspicions were confirmed when I found out that the employer, a small business owner, made his editorial staff pay for their own coffee and expected everyone to work on weekends, every weekend. Still, did I let a little thing like that or finding the managing editor crying in the bathroom stop me from saying yes? Hell, no. They were impressed with my credentials and told me everything I wanted to hear. I rationalized my decision by telling myself that it paid well, was closer to home, and was in a field that I had studied in college. Besides, how could you beat Monterey? It was a place they wrote songs about and had windswept cedar trees, fog, and two antique shops on every corner. What I find troubling is that I took this job knowing that it wasn't right for me and wouldn't last. Not only that, but even though I like antiques, I couldn't afford anything beyond a wooden pepper grinder, so it didn't matter how many antique shops there were. I did it, because I wanted to tell my previous employer to take a flying leap from a burning trapeze. Pride goeth before a fall (Proverbs 16:18).

It was a big fall. I lasted six months before they fired me. It was the only job I have ever been fired from. Well, not exactly. There was that one job right out of college at the Collegeville Flag Factory when I pressed so hard on the silk screens that I tore through four of them. They made all the flags right there, thus the name, and did the screening by hand (something about craftsmanship and quality). I'm sure they wanted to fire me since I couldn't do anything right (I would have fired me), but the owner's daughter liked me and must have pleaded with her father to let me stay. The father, obviously a clever man, agreed. He figured out I wouldn't be around much longer, and he was right.

Technically, I resigned my ill-fated editorial job in Monterey, although if I hadn't they were going to tell me sayonara, anyway. During my exit interview, which was done by Elsa, part owner of the enterprise along with her husband and "Chief Operating Officer" (it actually said that on her parking spot), I told her everything that was wrong with the place. I felt it my duty to represent the workers and stand up for their rights, even if they weren't willing to do so. I had a funny feeling about it, though. I thought of Actaeon being torn apart by his own hunting hounds. Elsa looked hung over but generally sympathetic.

"*Coffee?*" she repeated as if trying to understand the word.

"That's right. It should be free, especially when you expect people to work so many weekends."

"What else?"

"Well, there's no appreciation for the amount of work that goes on and the pride and professionalism of the staff," I said smoothly.

I had rehearsed what I was going to say during the commute from Santa Cruz to Monterey with my coworker, an attractive blonde with a quick wit and silver earrings who one day happened upon her husband and his gay lover in the bedroom of their home. They were getting divorced and I was treated to salacious updates every morning during our commute.

Elsa looked at me, trying to focus and dangling a number two pencil above a yellow pad. She hadn't written anything down.

"I see," she said.

"And what about Jonathan?" I asked, going for broke.

"What about him?"

"He's a nervous wreck."

"What can I do about that?"

"Give him the weekends off."

"We can't, we're under a deadline."

"We're always under deadlines. That's because we don't have enough time to get organized and Ray keeps changing assignments, layouts, and the editorial calendar. It's as if he tries to sabotage us."

Ray, her husband, was retired military and a workaholic, alcoholic, rage-aholic, talk-aholic, control-aholic, and probably choc-aholic, although I can't be sure about that last one. He had the whole "-holic" thing down pat. He was a big man with an expansive chest and a deep voice. Cavernous, you might say. They had met when he was stationed in Kaiserslautern, Germany and she was a barmaid in one of those traditional German dresses called a *dirndl* that make a woman look like she's either selling hot chocolate or staring in a porn movie; maybe selling hot chocolate *in* a porn movie. Elsa was not that kind, although she had an understated sensuality that made you take notice. It made me take notice, even while giving it. Whenever Ray recounted the story of how they met, he always said that she made him feel like Christopher Plummer. The base must have been throbbing with the sound of music.

"Jonathan is a grown man and has worked at this company for eight years. I'm sure if there had been a problem he would have told us," Elsa said.

"He cries in the bathroom."

"And what of it? I cry in the bathroom."

She was right. I could see that she had probably been there before coming to the interview. Her eyes were puffy and red. It couldn't have all been from binge drinking. The anxiety of conducting the interview could have sent her over the edge. After all, it was the first exit interview they ever did, which I thought strange considering the turnover rate was something like eighty-five percent. They couldn't keep anybody worth keeping, and the ones they did keep were a bit off. I'm thinking of Faisal, the Pakistani computer geek who helped us whenever static electricity caused the data on our eleven-inch floppy disks to disappear, which happened a lot. Yes, eleven inches. They weren't disks so much as personal pizza boxes. All it took was taking your shoes off at your desk and touching the metal drawer with your sock, so most of us sat perfectly still as we typed. Faisal wore short-sleeved shirts opened at the neck to show off his undershirt, stared at you forever without saying anything, and, on those rare occasions when he came down from stationary orbit, went on and on about how he was a member of Mensa.

"Isn't that a breath mint?" I asked once, rubbing the metal drawer with my sock.

"You know perfectly well it isn't."

"Oh, right. It's a Latin dance club."

"I have to go now."

"Thanks for your help."

Faisal lasted longer than me, a lot longer. And that was just one job among many. There were others that shouldn't have been but were, ranging from the improbable to the impossible. Some were outright absurd. Whenever I think of them and the people who were stuck in them like souls wandering through Limbo, I cringe. I cringe a lot nowadays. Memory can be a horrific thing. I'm not one to make light of Alzheimer's or any other disease where you lose your memory, but I think it can be just as painful to realize that something you remember is gone and that you can never relive it or change what happened. You can remember, but other than that, there's nothing you can do about it except lie. And ever since Watergate, we've all come to understand that the cover-up is worse than the crime.

At one point, I sold insurance, which fit me about as well as a tight, polyester leisure suit. I know this, because I owned a yellow one in college that my mother bought at Sears after much pleading. Anyway, the first tipoff should have been the state insurance exam, which I passed not by studying California insurance law but learning how to identify key words, phrases, and numbers in the test questions. For instance, if the phrase "indemnity," "misrepresentation," or "liquidity" appeared in the question, the correct answer was (b). If "13%," (c). If there were questions with option (e), then (e) was the right answer. I have no idea how they worked that out, but a monkey could have passed the exam. The securities exams known as Series 6, 7, and 22 were harder. For those, the company didn't have any cheat sheets, so you had to study your tail off. People often failed the first time around. I passed the 6 right away but had to retake the 7 and 22. It didn't take long for me to realize that I was more enamored of test-taking and certification than the job itself. It certainly beat selling Oldsmobiles, which is what I did while waiting for my licensing to come through.

The last straw was rushing to the regional sales meeting in Oakland, California, shooting the breeze with the other reps over Danish and coffee served in china with gilded trim, and then gathering for a talk by the head actuary from corporate headquarters. It was a very big deal and had been promoted for weeks by the regional sales director, who expected the entire sales force to attend. I grabbed a seat by the wall in the back of the room and looked up at the clock. The guy started at 9:00 am on the dot (actuaries) with a "brief" introduction to the statistical theory of mortality rates. Or it could have been a history of the statistical theory of mortality rates. Or an introduction to the history of mortality. I can't be sure. What I do know is that by 9:17 I couldn't take it anymore. As discretely as I could, I picked up my Samsonite briefcase, which has lasted me through a number of ill-fitting jobs, went to the men's room to splash water on my face, and walked out the front door never to return.

But you can only do that so many times when you've got a wife and three little girls in ruffles and curls who depend on you. Somewhere along the way, you learn to like mortality tables or at least put up with them until you think of a viable Plan B. Maybe it's also a matter of being realistic, of knowing that a certain job isn't going to work out *before* you take it, like dressing up in a gorilla suit or repossessing cars, which is what a college roommate of mine did. Sometimes you've got to suffer through it and learn the hard way, which is what I usually do (well, the suffering part), although age has tempered that quite a bit. But I still worry about my daughters, because I don't want them learning the hard way. I want them to do better than that. I sound like my mother here—and probably every parent who ever lived—but the truth is I don't want to protect my daughters from every bruise and scrape. That would be overprotective and controlling, not to mention impossible. They've got to learn from their own mistakes. I just don't want them making the ones I made. That, to me, seems dumb. We ought to learn from each other so that, even though we make mistakes, we don't keep making the same mistakes.[2] Cows don't even do that. Well, maybe they do, but that's why they're cows.

Speaking of cows, sacred ones in particular, I have to confess that one of my biggest mistakes was being a liberal arts major in college. It doesn't prepare you for anything, no matter what they tell you about the need for critical thinking, breadth of knowledge, and education versus job training blah, blah, blah, blah, blah. They're all lies. Sure, it's great to wax eloquent about *The Aeneid,* dialectical materialism, or Derrida's deconstruction of construction, but nobody's going to pay you for it, trust me. It makes for charming banter at cocktail parties and soirées (you might even get lucky with a starry-eyed film student), but after a while correcting somebody else's grammar, even if only in your head, gets old if not downright offensive. See, it's icing on the cake but not the actual cake. All it does is leave the poor student with two options: unrelated, less-than-meaningful jobs in Twinkie or gorilla suits, or

---

[2] For years, I toyed with the idea of putting up a chart in the house, maybe in the garage so as not to attract the attention of guests, with rows listing the mistakes we've made as a family and columns with our names. I figured going back a couple of generations would be enough. It would work like this: If a mistake had already been made, even though it happened fifty years ago, you weren't allowed to make it again. You'd have to come up with some other mistake, or—now here's an idea—not make one. The idea never really took off, though, since getting rid of mistakes is like "shoveling shit against the tide," as my mother says. Truthfully, it was more of a threat I would use as leverage against my teenage children.

graduate school. And, since most people don't want to go to college to do things like repossess cars, although Mike enjoyed it because he was high most of the time, a liberal arts degree dooms people to years of slavery in the academic salt mines. Professors love it, because they create mini-me's who worship them and even dress like them, which I've witnessed personally and found more than a little disturbing, although that was in a Religious Studies Department that boasted a Jewish, Wiccan professor by the name of Opal Kline (how many points on that star?). We were all so very enlightened then.

They'll be a ton of backlash about this, mainly in department meetings from people who drink out of NPR coffee mugs, but I have a duty to stand up for students just as I did for my oppressed coworkers in Monterey. Of course, it didn't work then and probably won't now, but I can't keep towing the party line, comrades. Besides, living in your parents' basement at forty-five isn't very attractive. The bohemian life ends at least ten years earlier. I don't think anybody in *La Bohème* or its modern equivalent, *Rent*, was over thirty except the landlord. The irony here is that I did not follow my own advice.

"Go to law school before you set out to be a writer. That way you'll have something to fall back on," my parents counseled.

"All right," I said, lying.

"Play the game, get tenure, and then you can write as much fiction as you want and still have a secured position," a colleague advised.

"I will," I said, lying.

I remember a question a woman in a temp agency asked me on that fateful day in August with the cubic zirconium after I had finished my bologna sandwich and crawled back out into the two hundred-degree heat of Fifth Avenue. Even Patience and Fortitude, the library lions, looked spent.

"I've reviewed your application and need to ask you some questions," the woman said, looking at me through her black-framed, rhinestone glasses with a mixture of pity and contempt. The corners of her mouth were upturned slightly in a twist. I wasn't sure if it was a twist of irony or lemon from the iced tea she was drinking, but she definitely wasn't what you could call warm, in spite of the temperature. Thank God the office was air conditioned. Behind her sat a dirty, plastic pot on a file cabinet with ivy spilling out, nearly touching the floor. It looked like it needed water, a lot of water.

"So you have a bachelor's degree from Ursinus College?"

"Yes."

"In English?"

"Yes."

"And a minor in Philosophy and Religion?"

"That's right."

She paused and I offered, "I wrote a paper on Whorfian semantics. It was in an Advanced Grammar class."

I don't know why, but somehow in my arrogance I had managed to convince myself that this was significant. It sounded desperate. She looked up with more pity than contempt, then back down at my paperwork.

"And I see from your application that you've worked at a children's amusement park where, apart from your regular responsibilities running the rides, you spoke French to the tourists from Quebec...a summer camp for blind adults where you played darts with the campers and took them boating and hiking—in a swamp...a golf course where you washed the balls dredged up from the pond by scuba divers...and selling ice cream from a truck, although that was only for—let me see—two weeks."

"I got stung," I said.

"Stung?"

"By a swamp fly as I leaned out the window to give a kid a creamsicle. I got a huge lump on my forehead. It was near that same swamp in South Jersey where the summer camp was."

Staring.

"My mother made me quit the job."

"And now you want to be a writer?"

It sounded absurd when she said it, and I remembered the time, not much earlier, when I sat in the Navy recruiter's office with my father. To make his point, the recruiter had taken out a huge manual with an anchor on the cover, slammed it down on the metal desk, and declared, "We need people to write these, you know!"

"Do you have any skills?" she asked.

"Skills?"

"You know, can you do anything?"

"Well, I…"

"Yes?"

I cleared my throat and ran through the inventory on my fingers. It wasn't as bad as I thought.

"I took metal shop in high school."

"Go on."

"And print and wood and auto shop, too. Oh, and photography."

"Well, that's impressive," she said, somewhat relieved. "So, can you do any of those things now?"

"*Now?*"

"I don't mean right now, but have you kept up those skills so that we can tell a prospective employer?"

Suddenly, I felt flushed. I thought of the wooden duck ornament with the twisted, misshapen head, the uneven tin ashtray, and the disassembled carburetor that I couldn't for the life of me put back together. Pieces of it were in a shoebox on a shelf in the garage. The Christmas napkins were nice, though.

They had a little, red Santa head in one corner and green holly in the other. Lame but nice.

"Not really."

"And at Ursinus?"

"I studied English literature and classical languages."

Back to staring.

"They don't teach skills in college," I added as an afterthought. I wasn't trying to be a wiseass. It just came out that way.

"No, I suppose they don't," she said, sitting back in her chair. Then she formed a bridge with her fingertips and kept tapping them together, studying me. I don't know how long this lasted, but it was long enough to make me squirm, which was probably the point.

"Tell me, can you type?" she asked at last.

My immediate reaction was to say, "Type what?" but I didn't. I looked past her to the ivy reaching down the file cabinet. I didn't want the interview to end, but it was obvious that it was over. I didn't have anything to offer that anybody wanted. To this day, I still wonder whether my life would be different had I answered "yes." But I didn't. I told her the truth. I comfort myself with the thought that eventually my impersonation of somebody who knew what he was doing would have been found out, maybe in dramatic fashion. I picture some employer calling all upset about the kid they sent over who doesn't know his ass from his elbow and what kind of temp agency are you running over there, anyway? And he would have been right. I didn't know how to do anything, not even type, which was ridiculous considering all the typing we had to do in our senior seminars. But I was a pecker, not a typer. I still am.

So, what would have been different, exactly? I don't know. But if I had had a practical skill—cabinetry, stained glass, copy machine repair, topiary design—I would have been able to pay the phone and electric bills on time and maybe afford a vacation to Mazatlan, where you can dive off the cliffs into an azure sea, which would have been something to write about. Hemingway went there to fish. I could have done that and then gone off to Spain to fight in a war. But then I also might have pushed my daughters into the liberal arts, the grass always being greener. Who knows, they could be starving artists in a drafty garret right now instead of well-paid professionals in California. I guess they'll just have to live with that shame and read *The Aeneid* in a good translation. I'll be there to help them.

Give Us Our Trespasses

This is a story about public speaking or, to be more precise, public recitation. By recitation, I mean standing up and reading off names the way they do every September 11 at the World Trade Center in Lower Manhattan. But the story that follows precedes September 11 and is in no way comparable to it other than that it involves a man standing up and reciting names. Beyond that, there is no similarity at all, so please do not assume that I am trying to make one. Nothing could be further from my mind. This is also a story about meaning and purpose and how, whenever you run into somebody who goes on and on about the importance of meaning and purpose as opposed to making money, you should run the other way, because you'll just be wasting your time. As the wise man sayeth, there is an appointed time for everything, and when you are young your time should be taken up with earning a living and providing for your family. Mine should have been, but thanks to an impulsive and idealistic nature (not to mention an affinity for smoking pipes and reading classical literature), I quit the aforementioned job with the insurance company, the bitter taste of mortality tables still in my mouth, and dove headfirst into meaning and purpose.

"Here's one," Heidi, my wife, said. "It's working with CYO and United Way. Maybe you could do that. They're hiring right now."

I won't go into the details of how a twenty-three year-old, Italian-American kid from New York City got married to an Austrian-American girl from San Francisco named Heidi whose mother's original language was German, but suffice it to say that it was the source of a great deal of friction and that singularity event I wrote about earlier. On the plus side, it was great for helping me find meaning and purpose even if not helping me put food on the table or winter coats on the kids. Good thing we lived in California. We had three girls, including twins, not quite two years apart (I don't mean the twins—that would be painful), which meant we had three little girls in diapers. I can still smell the urine in their bedroom every morning. Lena was our first-born, Rose and Deanna our twins. We decided to go with traditional family names instead of the flora of Yosemite or the moons of Jupiter, although Europa and Thebe probably would have gotten less of a reaction from friends than Lena.

"Oh, isn't that quaint. I had an Aunt Rose," people would say. That's what we were going for: quaint. The quaint twins were born nine minutes apart.[3]

---

[3] There is considerable disagreement as to the actual time separating the twins' birth. Heidi swears it was nine minutes, but then she was sedated with an oxygen mask over her face and her feet in the air. I say eleven but, since I am not exactly detail-oriented, I can't swear by it. The only other people in the room were the anesthesiologist and obstetrician, both of whom were too busy to take notice. I helped them, passing along surgical instruments like a pair of tongs and what looked like an eggbeater. You'd think they were making brunch. Total time from first contraction to first delivery was approximately two hours, with half an hour of that spent in the car getting to the hospital in Palo Alto. "Can't you drive any faster?" Heidi gasped between contractions. Footnote to the footnote: I am not a fast driver, never have been. Speed makes

"Longest nine minutes of my life," Heidi said.

"Oh, I dunno. How about the wedding vows?"

Wifely stare.

Let me begin my story by backing up, which I usually do, to a night not long after quitting the insurance company when I had already been deeply involved in the search for truth and reading a book about Buddhism. I had gotten it into my head that the search for truth should take me as far away as possible from the faith and spirituality I had grown up with, so I immersed myself in Eastern philosophy and short stories set in places with rice bowls, saffron, and bamboo groves. It was a dark and stormy night (it really was), the wind howled, and the branches of the redwood tree above our house swayed wildly. I was in bed with Heidi, reading about how life is like an onion and the point of a spiritual practice is to peel away the layers of illusion: appearance, intellect, personality, experience, political affiliation, etc. And, just like an onion, when you peel the layers away, you arrive at your inner core, the inner truth: nothing. See, the point of life is that there is no point at all, so stop trying to make sense of it with your Western, analytical mindset. Just sit back and enjoy the ride, because you're going to end up as dust that some termite will crawl over and take a crap on. There'll be nothing left of you, and eventually you'll be less than dust. I have to admit, it wasn't exactly uplifting. Just then, a gust of wind ripped off a huge redwood branch that crashed onto our roof. Then the electricity went out. I did what any self-respecting, American male would do: I screamed.

The next morning the doorbell rang.

"Good morning. We'd like to share the truth with you."

"What?"

---

me nervous.

"The truth."

"You want to share the truth with me?"

"Yes."

I ushered them in as quickly as possible. It was Saturday and I had been sitting at the kitchen table after clearing branches and debris from the storm. Still shaken from the revelation about nothingness, I decided not to go to the Buddhist temple in Watsonville, and now these three odd-looking people had shown up at my door. If I had gone to the temple, I would have missed them. I was convinced that this was a sign from God, *fato* even. But, as is the case with signs from God, I wasn't quite sure what it meant, which has been another one of my problems. Maybe it's the problem most people have: not so much questioning God's existence as trying to figure out what He's telling you. For me, that's the kicker. Actually, there could be a business opportunity here: Rosetta Stone for God.

"Please, have a seat," I said. "Coffee?"

They took tea instead, no cream or sugar. Apparently, they didn't want to be thrown off their game. They were Jehovah's Witnesses, JWs for short. They started right away with questions about my faith, the Bible, where I went to church, and how I lived my life.

"Lorna Doone?"

"No, thank you. So, have you ever thought about death?"

"Oh, all the time," I told them.

"What do you think about?"

"Onions."

"Onions?"

"Onions."

I took one from a basket on the counter and peeled it, telling them the story about nothingness and the branch crashing and the lights going out and how I screamed like a schoolgirl. They listened intently and then looked at me funny.

"Well, we don't have nothing inside us," Tim, the leader, said. "Uh, what I mean is, we have something inside us."

He had a very short haircut and a briefcase like my Samsonite. I wondered if there were mortality tables inside.

"That's right. We have something," his assistant echoed. She was a perky woman with a hairdo like Brenda Lee's, which was so out of fashion it looked punk. All she needed were a nose ring and eyebrow piercing. As soon as she told me her name, I forgot it. Elise, Eileen, Aileen, Helene, Maybelline?

"Well, then, what's left to discuss? Sign me up," I told them against my better judgement, crying from the onion.

And they did. Tim gave me a brochure, two issues of *Watchtower*, and directions for getting to the Kingdom Hall in Aptos, which he pulled out of his briefcase. When they finally left, I felt a lot better, which I figured was a good sign. I didn't say a word about it to Heidi when she got home. One thing at a time, I thought.

I lasted one month. I liked the smell of the ink and glue in their little, red books and how everything was ordered and neat down at Kingdom Hall, order being something I sorely lacked in my life. But something was off. I could feel it. It was the same feeling I had gotten at my editing job in Monterey. The hospitality minister with the gimp and cross-eye who met me at the door every Sunday morning didn't help. In the end, it came down to the Trinity, which for the JWs is a huge deal since they think it is a perversion of the one, true, Jehovah God (they went around saying "Jehovah God" like that was God's first and last name). But I couldn't believe that the entire Christian world was wrong and had been getting it wrong for the past two millennia, as if the JWs had some secret knowledge that nobody else possessed. So I researched it by reading everything I could get my hands on and talking to anyone who would listen, including the people who slept at the Santa Cruz Public Library. One bearded guy in Young Adult Fiction who smelled pretty bad went on and on about Gnosticism and then asked me if I had any weed. I don't know if you've ever googled "the Trinity," but there has been more written about it than anything else, once you get past the Keanu Reeves stuff. Then our family friend, Paul, a devout mechanic who read the *Summa Theologica* as he worked underneath cars, gave me a copy of Thomas Merton's *Seven Story Mountain*, which was the final nail in the JW coffin. I've never been to a JW funeral, but I'm pretty sure they're allowed to use pine coffins.

I feel compelled to bring up a point about JWs. They have made appearances at various times in my life but always during a low point or crisis. Just recently, my New York consulting business has experienced problems. Clients are hard to come by and getting the current ones to pay seems even harder. So who do you suppose have been springing up like mushrooms after a summer rain? No longer confined to the subway or street corner, JWs are turning up in unexpected places in bizarre ways. I don't argue theology with them anymore, having gotten over that need years ago. It's not what they say that challenges me now but the fact that they are everywhere. If their presence means anything, I have to ask again, what? Do they show up when I am about to fall over like expectant buzzards waiting to tear into my flesh, or are they meant to help me in some way? I realize I am attaching intention here, but I just can't believe this is all a coincidence. It has happened too many times. It's not what I call the "VW Syndrome," either, which refers to the time I bought my first bug and then noticed VW bugs everywhere I went. It isn't that. Their increased presence is real. I just don't know why. I suppose you could get all business school about it and ask, "What are the "takeaways?" But I won't. That would just add to the deterioration of the English language (compare with "evil doer" and the use of "impact" as a transitive verb).

This search for the truth had begun at the insurance company and took on urgency once I walked out that morning never to return. I was trying to make meaning and purpose profitable, but before I could do that, I had to figure out what it meant. What, exactly, was meaningful and purposeful for me? I knew it wasn't tax deferred annuities, but I had so many ideas in my head it was as if I had none. So, when the Trinity thing got resolved, I made a beeline to St. Joseph Parish in Capitola-by-the-Sea, where it just so happened they were hearing confessions. I went in, knelt down, and recited the prayer taped to the wall. I told the priest everything that had been going wrong in my life, including the run of bad luck we had had regarding do-re-me and how Heidi had to pawn her recently deceased mother's costume jewelry to buy milk for the kids. Then she ran out of gas on the freeway. A Highway Patrol officer stopped to help, picked her and the kids up, and took them to a gas station, whereupon she promptly spilled gas all over the floor of his patrol car. And about the guy who had been living with us from the insurance company whose wife left him on the beach in Monterey when he went into the water for a swim. Left him with nothing but a bathing suit, beach towel, and $2.33 in change in his shoe. So he stayed with us until Heidi thought his showering for thirty minutes and walking around in nothing but a towel eating granola in front of the girls was a bit much. I didn't have any big-time sins to confess, not having murdered anybody (I had thought about it), and for my penance the priest asked me to pray for him. I thought that was a bit odd but did it anyway.

So we started going to church to find meaning and purpose in our lives. Heidi was much more open to St. Joseph's than Kingdom Hall, which I eventually had to tell her about since Tim kept calling the house. It was either that or make up a gay affair, which I considered. Ironically, St. Joseph's was the same church we had gone to just after moving to Capitola from

San Jose. The move coincided with the editing job in Monterey, which I have written about, and was about as painful as having your wisdom teeth pulled out, which also happened to me at this time, not that I had any wisdom to spare, but that's the way things work. And as long as we're on the subject of the way things work, I might as well confess that I have found more evidence to support the belief that life is absurd—simply absurd—than that it involves some grand scheme or design. If that's true, then God isn't a person, place, or thing but a great guffaw and slap on the back, but I am getting ahead of myself.

We moved to Capitola in early December and spent our first Christmas in the new house with Heidi's grandmother, who came up from San Diego. We had visited her the previous summer during a trip to Disneyland and Sea World with the girls. Paul, our mechanic friend, had given us $200 in cash to help with the trip, which we took in our 1978 Volkswagen Bus. We barely had enough money to get there, visit the two theme parks, spend time with family sleeping on the floor and couches, and drive back. While in San Diego, the starter died and I didn't have money to replace it, not even with a refurbished part. So I had to push the bus from behind with everyone inside to get wherever we were going. Heidi would sit at the wheel and jump start the engine. Once the engine kicked in and the bus started moving, I'd race alongside, jump in, and close the sliding door behind me. It only took a few times before grandma made us go to a mechanic to have the starter replaced. She paid for it "gladly."

On Christmas day we got up early, the girls opened their gifts, grandma, Heidi, and I had coffee in our pajamas, and I waited to use the bathroom. And waited. By the time we got in the bus, which I mentioned several times to grandma was a joy to drive now that I didn't have to start it like Fred Flintstone, it was nearly noon. We needed gas and the right rear tire was leaking, so I drove down to the gas station with everybody to take care of the leak. That's when I realized I had no idea where we were going and hadn't made any plans (that detail thing again). At least the station was open. This was a time when gas stations had phone booths and phone booths had phone books. They were called "yellow pages," mainly because they were yellow. I went to the booth and tore through the yellow pages, looking up "Churches." There was a Seventh Day Adventist church across the street, which would have been perfect, but it was closed. All of the churches were done for the day except one. As it turned out, it was St. Joseph, which had a Mass at 12:15 pm, which was perfect. I returned to the bus, where they were all waiting for me in their Sunday best, both proud and relieved that I had managed to pull this one out of my hat once again. Way to go, dad, you're the man!

That was our introduction to St. Joseph. Later, once Heidi had agreed to start going with the girls, it was time to jump in with both feet. That's another one of my eccentricities, which I prefer to think of as endearments—you know, those little things that make us the unique human beings that we all are. One of mine is that if I am going to do something, I have to do it, to quote Frank Sinatra, all the way. That is, if I'm going to get into the boat, I do it with both feet. So we decided to commit ourselves seriously to church, which had the unintended effect of making me very critical of anything that didn't offer ultimate meaning and purpose, or at least attempt to. Why spend your money on what is not bread and your labor on what does not satisfy? For me, the biggest part of my life that did not satisfy was my job. I know a lot of people don't find their jobs satisfying, and if you ask them why they work, they'll show you pictures of their spouse, kids, or Bighorn fifth wheeler. It was the same for me until the day Heidi found the CYO (Catholic Youth Organization) job. As a kid, I had played on teams with CYO and the Police Athletic League, so I was familiar with how they worked, not that that qualified me to run the entire operation, but that's just what happened. I walked in one day and they hired me the next. That was another sign right there. With God behind it, what could possibly go wrong?

Meaning and purpose come in all sizes just like disasters, pizza, and women. I am not implying anything here beyond variety, and I don't necessarily equate women with pizza or disasters. I also do not mean to suggest that there were pieces of flotsam floating around in my new-found faith life, either; it's just that I learned to appreciate things I never even noticed before, like Scouting. I have never been a Scout, although I think I would have looked good in blue. Neither was I in the military. The closest I have come to a uniform is Little League and Pop Warner. I have a dear friend who was a member of the Hungarian Scouts in Los Angeles, which may or may not be a neo-fascist group, but he is a great guy who happens to detest Communists, having escaped Budapest in 1956, which was a good year for that sort of thing. Later, he volunteered to serve in Vietnam even before the draft board got ahold of him.

Let the record show that I believe in Scouting. I believe it strengthens the social and moral fabric of our society as well as the psychological and physical condition of boys and girls. It is a laudable tradition with a decorated history and is as American as apple pie (I understand the French have *green* apple pie). I just never knew it had anything to do with church, but it does. Not only does it have to do with church, but, more to the point of the story, it had to do with my job. In my official capacity as the CYO Program Director, I was responsible for working with a volunteer committee to put something on called the Catholic Scouting Awards ceremony. No, I am not putting you on. I wasn't aware of Catholic Scouts, let alone an awards ceremony. But such a thing existed, and it took place once a year. As it happened, the year was coming up just as I began work at the diocese, which is the local church headquarters. The bishop referred to the diocesan office as "that place from which a thousand indecisions have been launched" (819 were his).

"So, the first order of business now that the bishop has confirmed the date and time of the awards ceremony is to find a parish," announced Eduardo at the committee's first meeting. Then he sat back quite satisfied and sipped his caffè macchiato.

Eduardo was one of the representatives from the Boy Scouts. Originally from Argentina, he worked as a software engineer for Intel. Everything he said sounded as if it came out of the mouth of Count Dracula. There was a rumor that he had lived in a castle that had been converted into a hotel in Córdoba, which might explain why he always wore a blazer with a silk handkerchief. There was another rumor about him having been a gaucho at one time, but I think that was just the Mexicans making fun of him.

"We have the perfect place—our parish, Holy Spirit," Cheryl said.

Cheryl was from the opposing camp: the Girl Scouts. I hadn't realized it at the time, but there was a contentious rivalry between these two groups; maybe not among the troops themselves but certainly among the adults serving on the awards committee, which was composed of representatives from the Boy Scouts, Girl Scouts, Big Brothers, and Big Sisters. The committee awarded, among other things, the *Parvuli Dei* and *Ad Altare Dei* awards for boys, the "I Live My Faith" award and Marian Medal for girls, and the St. George Medal and St. Elizabeth Ann Seton Medal for adults. In addition, the ceremony included special recognition of individuals and groups who "served the cause of Catholic Scouting"; a flag blessing; processions; and an elaborate reception afterward with ice sculptures and live music from a mariachi band. It was what you'd get if you crossed Confirmation with an ROTC commissioning ceremony. People dressed up for it as if it were a wedding.

"No, we can't have it at your parish. It must be at Saint Michael's," Eduardo insisted.

"Why?"

"Because last year we had it at Saint Lucy's, which is Barbara's parish, and she is with the Girl Scouts."

"So?"

"So, it is logical to assume that this year we must have it at a parish with a large Boy Scout presence."

Eduardo always brought up logic. Engineering was logical, so he applied computer logic to every difficulty in life, including those encountered by the committee. He characterized opposing views as incorrect and flawed, since any argument made against logic must be—*ipso facto*—illogical and therefore not worth listening to. He usually did not resort to this argument until later in the meeting, but I found out from George, another adult leader, that he did it at the first meeting to impress the new program director.

"Well, that's just not going to happen!" Cheryl fumed. "We've had it at Boy Scout parishes for four of the past five years, and we've got to be fair to the girls and their families."

"But you don't have the numbers to support it."

"We've got more award winners than you do, and the bishop has said he wants to encourage the use of parishes that have been overlooked in the past."

"Holy Spirit has been overlooked?"

"Yes!"

"You are in the Northwest Deanery where there have been more catechetical dinners and CYO sports programs than anywhere else in the diocese."

"That's not true!"

"Of course it is. The facts don't lie. Logic dictates that the ceremony be held at Saint Michael's."

"Is that so?"

"Yes, that is so."

"Well, let's just see what the bishop wants."

They both looked at me, followed by George, Barbara, and Paul, a pale kid with acne in an Eagle Scout uniform. He looked like he masturbated a lot, although I thought that was supposed to clear your skin.

"I'll check," I said, clearing my throat and trying to sound official. "This hasn't come up in my meetings with him yet. But shouldn't we check to see if the pastors are available? We can't really hold a ceremony of this magnitude without the pastor being there, right?"

I had no idea what I was talking about, but I had picked up enough after a month of meetings to know that the pastors wielded a lot of weight. They were clearly the clients in the entire "consumption process" (I learned that phrase in business school, where they actually use it with a straight face and hold day-long seminars on "How To Digitize the Consumer Decision Journey." No, I'm not kidding). What was being consumed in this consumption process? Not meaning, purpose, or even faith, but power. The pastors made the decisions and controlled the purse strings. The committee knew it, too.

"Well, that is logical," Eduardo conceded.

"Father Gary is on retreat but he gets back next week," Cheryl said.

"All right, then, why don't we wait until the next meeting to decide where we're going to hold the ceremony? We have two possibilities: Saint Michael's and Holy Spirit," I said.

"What if it works out for both of them?"

"We'll let the pastors decide."

Eduardo shrugged, slurped his macchiato, and sat back again. Cheryl simmered down a bit but did not look happy.

"Let's move to the next item on the agenda."

"That's me," George said, straightening his legal pad and leaning forward. "We need an emcee, somebody to introduce the bishop, the pastor, and the troops and to work with the liturgist so that things run smoothly."

"I've got the perfect person!" Cheryl blurted out.

"Good, because I was about to say that we don't have anybody yet."

"Who is it?" Eduardo asked, suspicious.

"Sara Moore from the local ABC affiliate. She's a former Girl Scout and an active member of Saint Patrick's. Wendy Silbers knows her personally and can extend the invitation. You know Wendy, don't you, Barbara?"

Barbara, a quiet woman with thick lips sitting next to Cheryl, adjusted her glasses, licked her lips, and nodded.

"She'll do a terrific job," Cheryl declared.

Thankfully, there was no objection, so George went on.

"We also need a reader, someone to call out the names of the award recipients. This is an important job, since this person can make the ceremony run smoothly or turn it into a total bore."

Cheryl snickered, Eduardo swirled his mocha, and the kid stared blankly. Then, suddenly, they looked at me. I felt a flash of terror. They couldn't possibly be thinking of me, could they? I didn't even own a summer suit. I did have a white sports coat that made me look like a waiter, although I preferred to think of myself as Humphrey Bogart in *Casablanca*. Whenever I wore it I would suck on my gums and make comments about transit papers.

"So, do we have anyone in mind?" I asked.

"Last year it was——" Eduardo began.

"A total disaster!" Cheryl interrupted. "I don't care who we get as long as it's somebody who can read and has stage presence. Not too much—we don't want to upstage the bishop—just enough."

"What about Amy Dunston from Catholic Charities?" Barbara asked timidly.

"Oh, she would be perfect!"

"No, we already have Sara Moore," Eduardo said. "We need a man."

Cheryl grumbled but didn't say anything. Then George said, "How about Stanley Cross from Toastmasters?"

"He would be terrific," Eduardo said. "He's the best public speaker I know and has a way with names. They roll off his tongue like water off a duck's you know what. He must be a linguist, I'm telling you."

"Well, then, how could we go wrong, I'm asking you?" Cheryl said with more than a pinch of sarcasm. I have to admit, I was growing fond of these two.

Satisfied, they turned toward me, but I had no idea and wouldn't have been able to tell the difference between Stanley Cross and Hugo Boss even after checking out the duck's you know what. I knew about Stanley Cross hand tools, but this didn't appear to be the same guy. So I did what anybody else in my situation would have done.

"Well, with a name like Cross, it must be God's will!"

There, I did it again. Another one of my endearments is that I set myself up. You could say I set myself up for this or that particular thing (e.g., failure, a fall, heartache, injury, being taken advantage of), but the problem is worse than that. I don't just set myself up for specific things, I set myself up as a matter of course. It's a reflex. I am a member of the genus *homo*, the species *sapiens*, the subspecies *sapiens*, and the form *de-sum*, which, thanks to all that unprofitable language study I did in college, I know is Latin for "not-I" as in non-being or "flunky."[4]

I could have said "loser" and been done with it, but the only loss I have ever suffered has been at my own hands, which might make me a masochist but not a loser. I am an unintentional masochist. I hear my father calling out to me like the ghost of Hamlet's father, "You're your own worst enemy, son." Actually, he never called me "son," although once in a while he would call me "Don Ciccio," which is the equivalent of Sherlock in the expression, "No shit, Sherlock." Once, after I pointed out that he had moved to the desert in Las Vegas and so had no room to complain about the heat, he called me another name. Most often, though, he just called me Robbie.

Then there's this larger question, related to the Trinity, also beyond my ability to comprehend. It has to do with "meant to be." It goes like this: A lot of people believe in things that are "meant to be" and talk about them in precisely that way. You don't have to be a Country music fan to hear it. People are always saying how certain things are meant to be and others are not. What I find interesting is that those things that are meant to be are the things that have actually happened as opposed to the things that are not meant to be, which have not happened. If I were less gracious I would accuse these people of armchair quarterbacking. It reminds me of a college course I had in Eighteenth-Century English Literature (unlike Advanced Grammar, which had five students, this course had twenty-two students—it was required) in which we studied Alexander Pope

---

[4] Italian, the language with possibly the greatest number of insults, off-color remarks, and sexual innuendos, has several words to express the concept of "non-entity" or loser as in, "Hey, Luca's not stupid, he's just a *pedalìno*." Literally translated, *pedalìno* means "sock." You could also use *calzètta* or *lòffio*, which means "flabby." Apologies to anyone with those words as last names. Italian, while beautiful, is often cruel.

and one of his interminably long poems at the end of which he says, "Whatever is is right!" Really? I never expected Alexander Pope and Country singer Alan Jackson to have anything in common besides being on Facebook, but there it is. Now that I think of it, Jackson does have that incredibly poetic line about the Chattahoochee being "hotter than a hoochie coochie." I bring this up, because I do not think my being my worst enemy is meant to be any more than driving on the right side of the road is meant to be. It is completely arbitrary and, being arbitrary, can be undone. People in lab coats are making discoveries every day about how we can reprogram our DNA to become different people, even as we sleep. Well, I'm not sure about the sleeping part. I think I saw that in a late-night commercial about coral calcium, but the idea that I am stuck with setting myself up is just that: an idea. I can decide to put it out of my head by replacing it with another idea any old day of the week. It's kind of like quitting smoking that way and just as easy.

However, a problem arises when you say things like, "Well, then, how could we go wrong?" or "It must be God's will!" You're basically setting yourself up again, jeopardizing all the hard work that went into reprogramming your double helix. Whether or not my DNA has been reprogrammed, I cannot say, although that brings up a different philosophical question regarding whether or not people really change. I've heard a lot of arguments on both sides but am still unsure. I know that a friend of mine, a recovering alcoholic, swears on his mother's bingo chips that he is a changed man, but then he gets addicted to one thing after another, from video poker to gardening to pot smoking to writing books on deconstructing business memos. He insists he is not an alcoholic. And he isn't. I'm just not convinced he's really changed.

St. Paul says that we have to become new creatures, be born again, if we want a new spirit. Whenever I hear that I think of Nicodemus trying to crawl back into his mother's womb. It's almost comical. Can we really put on "the new man or woman?" I don't know. I'm still working on the old one. One thing I am certain of, though, is that as we get older we become more of who we are, not less. So, if I am supposed to put on a completely new man, I'd better do it as soon as possible. I should have done it years ago; it may be too late now. But wait—after you put on the new man, what happens to the old one? Does he disappear completely, or does he hang around like a bachelor uncle after Thanksgiving dinner? I need to know not just for my sake but for my children's and their families.

I've already confessed that I am not detail-oriented. However, I am very observant and can pick up things that fly under other people's radar. I just can't arrange them in a way that makes much sense. So, you could say that I am detail-oriented in an abstract but not practical way. But aren't details practical, you ask? Maybe, maybe not. It sounds contradictory, but I notice peculiar things about people and places that would occur only to a compulsive neurotic, not that I am one, but I exhibit some of the behavior from time to time. I wish I were detail-oriented in a practical way and could account for the exact number of cents in an Excel spreadsheet, or blocks that the perplexed Belgian tourist has to walk before arriving at Columbus Circle, or steps seven through twelve in downloading the program to make the other program work so that I can get back to the grading rubric that was sent to me by an "education specialist" (whatever that is) to grade a student's essay. Whether or not the student learned anything other than how to manipulate the system is another question, one that education specialists never seem to get around to asking, let alone answering. But that's another story.

I may be off topic, but this leads me to another observation about details: they tend to obscure the real issues.

Now, don't get me wrong. I am not talking about the guy who works on your car or the pilot of the airplane you will be taking to St. Louis in July (seriously, have you been to St. Louis in July?). Those involve details that have a cause-effect relationship to reality, as in life and death, and I don't want anybody with their head in the clouds flying an airplane—well, you know what I mean. Our mechanic friend was an outlier who could work on your transmission while discussing St. Augustine's concept of the psychological Trinity (there's the Trinity again). Of course, cars didn't exactly fly in and out of his shop the way ideas flew in and out of his head. I still have a car there; dropped it off ten years ago. I'm not kidding. He told me he'd get to it when he finished Chesterton. I thought he meant a cigarette.

So we ended up going with Stanley Cross from Toastmaster's who, by the time of the ceremony, was now a golden-tongued orator in my mind, as well as the committee's. Without having met him, I began thinking of him as a contemporary John Chyrsostom, the fourth-century Archbishop of Constantinople, whose name, translated from Ancient Greek, means "golden-mouthed." The praise heaped on him by Count Dracula, George, and others, along with Cheryl's acquiescence (it could have been disgust) had me in awe of the man weeks before the ceremony. Perhaps that is overstating the case, but not too much. I probably would have had a healthier and more realistic attitude had I been able to vet him, but I relied on the good will and judgment of the committee. I also didn't have time to schedule an audition. What would that have looked like, anyway?

"Well, Stan, can you read this menu out loud from the Pho Hoa Restaurant across the street? And, please, take your time."

I was also bombarded by the demands of a project that would have rivaled a royal wedding: medals, awards, trophies, lists of kids from the participating parishes, seating charts, troop flags, pastor schedules, wheelchair accessibility, last minute changes to the liturgy (up to twenty minutes beforehand), ordering the food, sending out invitations, publicizing the event in the local media, getting the Knights of Columbus to show up in their capes, feathers, and swords, coordinating with the onsite staff at Our Lady of Sorrows (Eduardo and Cheryl both lost), and talking daily to the calligraphist (yes, calligraphist) so that she had the latest list of awardees for the certificates, which numbered about two hundred. At that point, it might as well have been two hundred thousand, because it had become a ridiculously complicated project with committee members throwing hissy fits at every meeting. Toward the end, it was twice a meeting. By the day of the ceremony, I thought *I* deserved an award.

The ceremony was scheduled for 3:00 pm on a Saturday in April after Easter but during the Easter season so that Our Lady looked a little less sorrowful with flowers and lilies and a new Easter candle made of beeswax in the sanctuary. The butterscotch smell of the beeswax filled the entire church. Despite the name, it was a new parish with an open air design and a circular nave surrounding the altar, which was more like a table than an altar. It was the kind of thing that drives traditionalists crazy, since they want that old time religion with blood sacrifices and plenty of "Lord, I am not worthy," while the younger, hipster types want a table where everybody sits around and, like, chills and sips wine.

I wasn't so concerned about the theology of the interior space as I was about being able to match the certificates that the bishop handed to each awardee with the list of names read by Stanley. To my detail-challenged mind, it seemed about as complex as landing a spacecraft on one of Jupiter's moons (Jupiter again). I had to provide Stanley with a list that matched the order of the kids coming up to receive their award and the certificates being handed to them by the bishop. So, that meant synchronizing three things: (1) Stanley's list, (2) the troops in the pews, and (3) the certificates. Given the chaos of troops, Knights, flags, parents, guests, and a roving photographer who kept asking if there would be an open bar, I might as well have been calculating percentages for liquid hydrogen. By 2:30 I discovered, to my horror, that the certificates the calligraphist had delivered were about twenty names short.

Enter Heidi, stage right. Oddly enough, she had just ended her rock painting class and taken up calligraphy. It was one of those things that you do on a whim while you're in between things, like the time, years later, when I ordered a home security system while waiting for a ride from my daughter. To this day, I'm not sure why she did it (or why I did it), and she hasn't done calligraphy since then. It was as if she had signed up for it in anticipation of the awards ceremony. If this wasn't divine providence, I don't know what was.

"Heidi, did you bring your pen and ink?"

"Yeah, they're in the car, why?"

"Can you fill out some certificates?"

"Sure, but I need the names."

"Got'em right here," I said, handing her the updated list.

Dutifully, Heidi got to work in the back of the church, setting up in the last pew with her wooden box of pens, ink bottles, and stained rags. The girls sat with her in their freshly-pressed dresses, fidgeting and running back and forth to the water fountain in the vestibule. When they knocked over one of the bottles, spilling ink on the pew, I managed to contain myself. I had brought extra certificates, which was a good thing, because as troops arrived with their harried adult leaders, I was handed last-minute changes and spelling corrections. I barely had enough certificates to cover the need, and we ended up with only two to spare, one partially filled out as a do-over. As the church filled up, we had to keep people out of the pew, because we needed room to dry the certificates. Heidi was still writing out names when the procession began.

The flag blessing took forever, because there were more flags than a Fourth of July parade and some of the kids had a hard time handling the poles. When it was finally over, I delivered the list to Stanley, who took his place in the sanctuary next to the adult leaders. He and Sara Moore were the only ones in civilian garb. Apart from the priests, who wore liturgical vestments, the rest had donned uniforms with bright cravats, one adult Scout sporting more medals than Leonid Brezhnev on the Kremlin reviewing stand. The scene looked colorful and the church was full, which was a good measure of success. I had been advised to have a big turnout for the bishop, who liked splashy events with a lot of people and no glitches (as opposed to no people and a lot of glitches). I sat down with Heidi and the girls in the back of the church, relieved that we had liftoff and all systems were go.

Now, I've lived in the Bronx, East 187th Street, by the zoo. I know how important it is to be on your guard at all times, even when, perhaps especially when, there is no imminent threat or danger. There's an element of the Law of the Jungle at work here (speaking of zoos), and the harsh reality is that if you let your guard down, even for a moment, you are exposing yourself to—someone might even say setting yourself up for—an attack. So, don't do it. Be on your guard even at rest. It's a lot like living in a Mafia movie. You never know when Jimmy Six Toes will come charging through the door, guns blazing, and blow your head off. That's why I always sit facing the door in restaurants. I want to see what's coming at me, whether Jimmy, the waiter, my ex-girlfriend's mother, or an out of control San Francisco Muni bus, which happens to look a lot like my ex-girlfriend's mother but without the mustache. Just remember that whoever or whatever it is, it'll always be a surprise. So, in a way, the one thing you can expect is the unexpected. Does that sound cynical? I don't mean it to be. It's just an observation I've made after having lived nine lives, and I'm not done yet.

So, what would be the most unexpected thing at this point in the story? Who do you suppose would come flying through the front door with a 9 mm Glock pistol in hand? Who's the last person you'd expect other than Jimmy Six Toes? That's the question you need to ask yourself. It was a question that, at the time, I was too naïve to ask, let alone answer. This breach in actionable information, as they say in the intelligence community, had disastrous consequences.

We had gotten to that point in the liturgy after the readings (don't ask me how they tied Scouting to the Book of Numbers) and the bishop's homily, which was about service and talents and how you can't bury either. The bishop had moved his hands a lot and his ring kept flashing, prompting a hundred questions from Deanna, who was the kind of kid who was curious about everything and asked more questions than a homicide detective. It was now time for the awards and certificates. Stanley, looking like a poet laureate, took to the ambo and adjusted the microphone with a graceful turn of the wrist, getting ready to read the names of the *Parvuli Dei* recipients. The bishop stood smiling, bouncing on the balls of his feet at the steps of the sanctuary, the parents leaned forward, hushed, and the photographer's camera went buzzing away. This, as they say, was the moment we had all been waiting for.

"P-P-P-eter Ad-d-d-ams," Stanley said.

A few coughs, then silence.

"J-J-J-oseph An-d-d-der-son."

It got even quieter.

"Ste-v-v-ven Ash-ash-ash…comb."

Heidi looked at me.

"Os-c-c-car Bet-t-t-t-en-c-c-c-ourt…"

I looked at Heidi, then the bishop, who began handing out the certificates as the kids came forward. I could see he was not amused and even turned to look at Stanley to see if this was some sort of joke. Unfortunately, it wasn't. Stanley was having a meltdown right in front of everyone. The gold-mouthed orator couldn't say boo without stuttering. I thought maybe it was the jitters and he would settle down once he found his stride. Well, he didn't find his stride or anyone else's, and the only thing that rolled off his tongue like water off a duck's you know what was you know what. I looked for Eduardo as if to get some explanation, but the count had vanished, presumably having turned into a bat and flown away. I could see the bishop scanning the assembly as if looking for someone to blame. That someone was me.

"T-t-t-rev-v-v-or D-d-d-ods-worth."

Stanley was in the "Ds" with a lot of names to go. People whispered, the pastor and the other presider laughed, and Stanley butchered every name on the list with abandon. It was actually beautiful the way, say, a train derailment is beautiful: horrifyingly so. Now, you'd expect Chinese, Czech, or Burmese names to be a problem, but he couldn't even say "Davis" in fewer than five syllables. It was as if he had never read a list in public before or stood at a podium. This was starting to be a screw-up of biblical proportions. When the certificates got out of order, which was the next thing to happen since at the last minute some kids hadn't shown up, the event turned into a circus. All they needed was a clown car. With the wrong certificate in hand, some kids stood there perplexed, others tried giving theirs back to the bishop, and still others began exchanging them as if they were trading baseball cards. I got a couple of adult leaders to go up and make their kids sit down, promising to sort things out later, but that only added to the chaos. By then, Stanley had gotten to the sweet part of the bat, which consisted of about forty-two Vietnamese names, which, if not for the generally good-natured disposition of the Vietnamese families, could have resulted in another Tet Offensive. As it was, it was still a disaster, and I could see steam rising on the bishop's face from his neck to his forehead and purple zucchetto, which I expected to go shooting off his head like a bottle rocket. There were now more people in the mix than the last scene of *Hamlet*, and it was just as bloody. "The sight is dismal..."

By the time Stanley got to some Polish kid whose name started with "S," I was exhausted. Sitting there powerless watching your career circle the drain and then make a sucking sound as it goes down is not a good feeling, particularly when it happens in front of your wife and kids. Not only was I exhausted, but I was wet with sweat and stained with ink from when I had jumped up at Stanley's pronunciation of a name that sounded like "p-p-penis." Most others had heard it, too, because it got a laugh from the troops (the girls more than the boys). Stanley p-p-powered on, though, seemingly unfazed by the carnage he was leaving behind. At a certain point, I even admired him for his ability to withstand utter humiliation. It takes strength of character to do that. And lack of intelligence.

Miraculously, we stumbled through the rest of the liturgy, which went off without any other catastrophes and was even, dare I say, prayerful. It was like the calm that follows an earthquake or tornado. Even the bishop settled down, and I began to think that maybe, as a man of God, he would show compassion and not fire me. I couldn't be sure, though. He may have been a man of God, but he did not suffer fools, and I'm afraid I was a fool. At least I felt that way. After what had happened, how could I not? Which brings me to another cosmic consideration: I am awful at everything. Most of the jobs I've had I either couldn't do or didn't care to do. I don't know if that describes three-quarters of the adult workforce, but it certainly describes me. I felt desperate again, but then something amazing happened. I had my first lesson not just in ministry but in the importance of relying on others, of community.

"I'd like to thank all of you for your participation in this ceremony and in the life of the Church," the bishop said, taking a moment out of the final blessing even though we had gone over our allotted time by a half hour.

"And, again, I offer my heartfelt congratulations to the Scouts, their families, friends, and supporters."

Before he could finish and escape to the outdoor buffet (artichoke cheese squares, Mediterranean quesadillas, and Pinot Grigio—a lot of Pinot Grigio), a Filipino woman stood up. She wore a white lace mantilla and raised her gloved hand like a traffic cop. I expected the worst but at this point cared the least, which might describe a lot of things, from post-traumatic stress to combat to marriage.

"Your Excellency, please, if you would indulge me, my daughter would like to say a few words of thanks on this very special occasion. She just received her first Scouting award and is very excited."

I could see a vein in the liturgist's neck burst, but then the bishop, with all the polish and political adroitness of a Clinton, glided over to the woman and said, "Is this your daughter?"

"Yes, your Excellency."

"And what is your name, dear?" he asked, leaning toward the girl, who couldn't have been more than ten.

"Rosalyn."

"Well, Rosalyn, what would you like to say?"

There was a pause, and I decided right then and there to walk out if she told him she got somebody else's certificate by mistake. But she didn't. She curtsied and said for everyone to hear, "I made a friend today and I wanted to thank you for it."

"A friend?"

She nodded, and you could hear the photographer's camera buzzing like an excited swamp fly. *My* swamp fly.

"And where is your friend?"

The girl pointed to another little girl about ten rows back, who stood up on the padded kneeler and waved excitedly.

"And this is the first time you met?"

"Yes, and it was all because everything was so mixed up that we had to talk to each other to trade our awards."

"I see."

"And that's when we found out that we go to the same school. So now we're friends. Her name is Alicia."

"I am so glad to hear that," the bishop said as the assembly applauded. Then he blessed the girl and her mother before returning to the altar, where, I swear, he looked directly at me.

I suppose it's true what they say about roses growing out of manure. There had been enough manure in the ceremony to supply a forty-acre mushroom farm for a couple of seasons. The bishop smiled one of his enigmatic smiles, also a mixture of roses and manure. I wasn't sure if it was a "we'll deal with this later" look, which is related to the "wait till I get you home" look, or something more insidious as in Donald Trump's "You're fired!" The only thing I knew for certain was that I had been spared final humiliation and defeat by a little girl in lace, who, in her innocence, had taught me a valuable lesson. What was that lesson? You've got to give other people their trespasses, because they're only human, and when you do that you just might find greater meaning and purpose than you ever expected. Hamlet said it best: "Our indiscretion sometimes serves us well." I consider myself well served.

Bloomington

If you're like me and somebody asked you to plot all the jobs you've had in your life, you'd no doubt come up with a very interesting graph of who you are and what you are about. Actually, I don't like that expression, "what you are about," ever since a melon-bellied professor of mine in suspenders as thick as seatbelt straps told me once that he had been discussing that very thing with a colleague concerning me. Apparently, the conversation didn't last very long, having been interrupted by a sales call from a textbook rep. I guess you have to set priorities. Nevertheless, looking at a graph or other visual representation of your employment history would be revealing, something that would cause you either to celebrate the rich tapestry of your life, or wallow in a frayed scatter rug of misery and regret. Of course, you could just get drunk and wrap yourself up like Cleopatra.

If I did my map, starting from my paperboy days in elementary school and busing tables in Wismer Dining Hall at Ursinus College, we would now be at the move from California to Maryland some twenty years later. It's a complicated map for the same reason that it's complicated for most people: it includes not just my employment history but my family and education. That is, my employment history is directly related to my education, although there is a twist to this, because the same was true for Heidi. We got married in a fever, to quote Johnny Cash, had three children by the age of twenty-five, and then decided to go back to school and figure out what we wanted to do with our lives. Backwards? Maybe. Difficult? Incredibly. Would I trade places with those forty-somethings who are just beginning to consider the possibility of maybe having a kid or two at some point in the not-too-distant future once things settle down and they have enough money saved in their defined pension plan but only after crossing off a minimum of three items on their bucket list, one of which is to live long enough to see Cher's actual farewell tour? Not on your life. I don't have a bucket list. For a long time, I didn't even have a bucket.

Heidi went back to finish her bachelor's degree and get a master's; I went for a master's and doctorate.

"You always have to go one better, don't you?"

"Not at all," I said. "But I have to get a doctorate. What else am I supposed to do with a master's degree in religious education?"

"Oh, I don't know—get a job?"

We met at the Paul Masson Champagne Cellars in Saratoga, California, where we both worked as tour guides and wine hosts in the tasting room. I remember the multimedia presentation accompanied by Vivaldi's *Four Seasons* that the visitors watched to start their visit. Afterward, they would go on the self-guided tour with remote control "wands" held up to their ears. They looked completely ridiculous. But the Vivaldi, grapes, oak barrels, and champagne bottling room made for a very romantic experience. I was attracted right away to Heidi's dark eyes, slim figure, and mullet. She thought I was strange, an Easterner with an accent who dressed "like a shoe salesman." Her first words to me were, "Get out of my way, you stupid idiot!" We were both coming to the swinging door of the kitchen in the tasting room but from opposite directions. She was pushing a cart of newly-washed wine glasses for the bar, so I promptly got out of her way. Then, enticed by her disdain and the possibility of pursuit, I got in her way. The absolute shortest version of this is that we got married in the aforementioned fever, had three children, and decided to go back to school to make something of ourselves. It's not really that simple and that's not the true order of things, but there's no need to get technical right now. It's not like I'm writing a Navy manual, although I understand they still need people to do that.

My work map up to this point looks like this: Central Penn Bank, Paul Masson Winery, the California Association of CPAs (accountants have manuals, too), *Central Coast Business*, Santa Cruz Oldsmobile, JP Hawthorne Insurance, the Roman Catholic Diocese of San Jose, and The Liturgy Congress in Washington DC (not to be confused with the Library of Congress). There's a lot that came after that, but this is a story about Bloomington, so I'll have to hold off on those other jobs for the time being, maybe put them in another book entitled *What Was I Thinking?* It'll be in three volumes. The Bloomington story begins with Heidi being accepted into the social work program at UC Berkeley and our decision to move into graduate student housing, which was affectionately referred to as "the Village." When I first heard it, I thought of Patrick McGoohan in *The Prisoner* being chased by that huge, white beach ball, which wasn't exactly comforting. The reality wasn't much better. The housing turned out to be refurbished Army barracks from World War II, and they put the five of us into a one-bedroom apartment that Lena still refers to as "the shack." We were nothing if not adventurous.

It was in the Village that we met the Nigerians.

They tell me that doing business in Nigeria is nearly impossible, that the government is corrupt, the infrastructure unstable, and their greatest natural resource—oil—vulnerable to fluctuating exchange rates on the international market. It can go anywhere from $35 to $135 a barrel and back down again, which isn't exactly a solid foundation for an economy. They also can't seem to figure out what to do with the money once they've made it. But they love education. In fact, they probably appreciate it more than we do, because if you have to walk six miles to go to school, you make sure it's worth your while. Of course, if you forget anything like your shoebox diorama of Queen Victoria's sitting room, you're pretty much up the Niger River without a paddle. So when we heard about this Nigerian family crammed into graduate student housing in the block next to ours, we knew they were serous. Just how serious I didn't realize until one day Rose came home and said, "Did you know Ngozi has five brothers and sisters?"

"Who?"

"Ngozi, my friend."

"That's strange. Usually, Japanese families are small."

"Dad, she's from Africa. I think they come from Nigeria. Mom knows them."

"They live in the Village?"

"Yeah, I just came from their place."

"Wait," I said, counting on my fingers. "Are you telling me there are six kids and their parents living in one of these apartments?"

"Not the father. It's just them and the mom."

"Seven?"

"Yeah."

"And who's the student?"

"I think it's their dad."

"Where is he?"

"Wyoming."

"Well, I can understand that. There's a lot of space there."

That evening I asked Heidi about it and, sure enough, it was true. She had met the mother at the Village Cafe and gotten to know them. Amanda was living in a one-bedroom apartment with her six kids, who ranged in age from fifteen-year-old Kemel ("Kenny") to a baby girl named Ebube whom everybody called "Buby." There were three others in addition to Ngozi, but the only one I could remember was a boy named Boma who had a smile wide enough to melt your heart and a personality to match. From what I could gather, the father was studying anthropology at Berkeley and had just gotten some kind of teaching position at the University of Wyoming, Laramie. I tried to picture eight Nigerians living in the sagebrush and sand of the high desert but couldn't quite do it. Little did I know that in a short time I wouldn't have to imagine anything, but I'm getting ahead of myself.

Over the next six months we got to know the Okafors. They were Roman Catholics like many Igbo families: devout, funny, and some of the most refined people I've ever met, the girl in my class at Ursinus who played the piano in a pair of white gloves notwithstanding. The kids attended the same middle school as our girls and were very serious about education. The curious thing about them, which was a lesson for us, accustomed as we were to personal space and privacy, was that they never complained about the living arrangements. A couple of times I tried to bait them, but they didn't bite. You had to see it to believe it: seven people living, eating, and sleeping in about three hundred square feet. I suppose it was what Francescoantonio had to endure, although his was even worse because of the harsh winters living in a walkup in New York City during the 1890's, but it still got to me. By then, we had moved up to a two-bedroom apartment on the second floor of the barracks with a nice view of a clothesline, but we were still complaining. Our friends back home thought we had lost our minds.

"Why give up your nice life in Capitola to live in a barracks in Berkeley?"

"Albany."

"Albany."

"For the adventure."

"What adventure?"

"You know, the poor student adventure."

"With three kids?"

"They're students, too."

This is where the Bloomington adventure begins in earnest. Several things had to converge at one point like that singularity event with Mother Matter I wrote about in "Angelina." Here's what converged: Heidi finished her degree in social work, I decided to go to graduate school in Washington, DC rather than stay in Berkeley, the Okafor father finished his degree and worked full-time in Wyoming, and Amanda and the six kids were getting ready to join him. That's a whole lot of convergence. Still, you need a catalyst to get it all moving. What we had so far were all these ingredients in a pot, but they needed stirring to make a stew. That stirring was our decision to take the northern route across the US, since we would be traveling at the end of July, early August, and had heard about people dying from the heat in places like Arizona and Texas. That meant we would be driving our 22-foot Penske truck and minivan on Interstate 80 right through Laramie, Wyoming. So, you could say the catalyst for all of this was hot air. You could also say that the stage was set for disaster.

The Okafors didn't have much furniture, but they had even less money (they subsisted on rice and fish), so we offered to help. Why not? We assumed that we had plenty of room for at least some of their furniture, and it was a great relief to Amanda the day I went to her apartment to offer help.

"We'll have room, don't worry about it," I assured her.

"That's so nice of you. Let us help."

"No, really. It's not a problem."

"We can't let you do all of that without paying you something."

"I won't accept any money."

"But I insist."

"No, really."

"But we have more furniture in storage and could use as much space in the truck as you are willing to give us."

"How much more?"

"Three rooms."

"It'll never fit," I said.

"No, but if you take as much as you can, we will pay you."

I am nothing if not principled, but the offer was tempting, especially since Heidi and I ran the numbers the night before and discovered that the move was going to cost a bundle. There were the truck rental, the extra insurance we decided to get (I've learned the importance of it over the years), gas for the truck and our own car, hotels, meals, and souvenirs from places like Little America with that big penguin overlooking the interstate. I remembered it from the days when my family took cross-country trips from Staten Island to San Jose to visit Aunt Frances and Uncle Frankie. Those were sojourns lasting five and six days with the station wagon packed to the roof, leaving us kids with about as much room as in a Mercury capsule, which was why my father threw a fit the time he found out I had packed the Staten Island phonebook (I must have a thing for phonebooks). What really sent him over the edge was my explanation about needing it for addresses to send postcards to my friends.

"Okay, you can have the back quarter of the truck. We'll fill up three-quarters with our stuff first and then load yours in last. That way, it'll be easier to drop off in Laramie."

"You see? A perfect plan," Amanda said, smiling. Then, after a thoughtful pause, "God provides."

On moving day I went with Kenny to the Penske store in Berkeley to pick up the brand new Ford truck they had reserved for us, which had all of sixty-three miles on it. Kenny served as my backup, parking, and logistics assistant, which meant telling me when I was five feet from the curb or about to take out somebody's rain gutters. What I discovered, which I already knew from a dozen previous moves, is that I am a terrible driver. There, I said it and am not ashamed of it. I don't like driving, because you have to pay attention not only to what you are doing but to what everybody else is doing. I can't handle that kind of pressure. I am usually thinking of other things or mesmerized by the monotony of white lines and taillights. If I'm on a highway that stretches for hundreds of miles without anything changing in the landscape, which describes most of the American Southwest, then it's all over. I don't like speed, either, as noted, so I have to stay in the right lane or risk being flipped off or worse. I also can't handle anything bigger than a minivan or small truck. I am in awe of people who drive buses, especially the articulated kind, and am terrified by the sight of a tractor trailer coming down the street and turning the corner in a densely populated metropolitan area like New York City.

It took all day to pack the truck. Besides the home regiment of Okafor kids and Brancatelli girls, there was Pilar, a sweet, pudgy girl with bifocals whose family came from Bolivia; Andrea, Lena's Greek-American friend from down the street whose father was a baker; Steve, a skinny, good-natured kid with wavy hair who had a crush on one or all of the girls at the same or different times; and the usual assortment of what I called the "Village People" (no Indian chiefs) who would come by to check up on things, move a lamp stand from one spot to another, or position themselves at the back of the truck to stroke their faces and study our progress. A geometrical formation was taking shape before our eyes consisting of tables, bed frames, box springs, mattresses, couches, chairs, desks, and box after box of clothes, books, dishes, appliances, picture frames, knick-knacks, bric-a-brac, and memorabilia that three teenage girls had managed to accumulate over the years. We also had to feed a small army, so Heidi acted as quartermaster, making runs to the local deli and grocery store for sandwiches, beer, soda, iced tea, cookies, doughnuts, and ice. Plenty and plenty of ice. When you're packing a moving van in July, you can't have too much ice.

By the time we loaded our things, the truck was nearly full, so we had to make some painful decisions about what to leave behind. Painful as in, "I'm not getting rid of that antique card catalogue with the brass handles."

"What, the one your old girlfriend gave you?"

"That was before you."

"Well, I'm not getting rid of my mother's credenza from the Philippines."

"You're mother isn't from the Philippines."

"I didn't say she was."

"It's ugly."

"No, it's not."

"I didn't mean the credenza."

You get the idea. To cut to the chase, the wrought-iron patio chair that I had fallen in love with over the years, Heidi's rattan chair that looked like a giant wok with a water-stained cushion that weighed more than the frame, the bookcase I had made by hand with the shifting center of gravity, the four boxes of Playskool toys—all gone, donated to the Village Thrift Shop. We kept this up until Amanda came by to ensure that there was actually twenty-five percent left. I even measured it with Kenny (five feet, six inches). Then we loaded their things, and I managed to pull down the louvered door of the truck and lock it. By then, it was seven-thirty in the evening.

"Well, there's no point leaving now. We might as well spend one more night and leave early in the morning."

"But what about the hotel?" Heidi said. "We'll lose our money. Come on, we can drive to Reno and then relax. We're at the Hilton. They have a pool."

"Pool?" Deanna repeated.

I looked at my daughter, who looked back at me with her big, brown eyes.

"All right, we'll go to the Hilton."

We said our goodbyes, which was very emotional with crying all around. Even though we had spent little more than two years in the Village, we had made very close friends. As we pulled away, the kids ran after us, waving and shouting, some on bikes. Ngozi and Boma were in the lead. It was like the departure of people leaving their homeland to seek a better life. I thought of Tom Joad and his trek westward to California and the *clandestini* making their way across the deserts of Libya to get to Lampedusa.[5] We were definitely on a mission for a better life, but I couldn't help feeling that we were losing something we would never get back. We had created a life for ourselves in the Village and university, a good life with friends and a routine and a network of relationships that enabled each of us to thrive. We were a family, and I don't think there was ever a time when we felt so close. I looked back in the side view mirror, watching the last of the kids as they pedaled frantically and waved in the twilight, knowing that this moment would never exist again. I thought of Goethe's *Faust*: *Verweile doch! du bist so schön!*[6]

---

[5] A great book for anyone interested in the "*clandestini*" is Fabrizio Gatti's *Bilal: Viaggiare, Lavorare, Morire da Clandestini* (Milano: RCS Libri, 2007). It's in Italian but probably has been translated by now. If I had an editorial assistant, they could look it up for you.

[6] *Faust 1, v. 1700:* "Stay a while; you are so beautiful." Faust was referring to that one moment in life so beautiful and sublime that, once experienced, you are ready to die. Then Faust met Margaret. Again, I apologize for the footnotes. Once, I added a footnote to my shopping list *while* shopping. It had to do with brands of green tea. I preferred White Rose over the

I followed Heidi, who drove the minivan with two of the girls and Fred, our parakeet named after Fr. Ed, a friend of the family (we can be very clever that way). Rose rode with me in the Penske, shotgun, which meant flipping through radio stations at the speed of an automatic weapon (maybe they should call it "riding Uzi"). We arrived in Reno five hours later, not bad considering we had to cross the Sierra Nevada Mountains, but then we discovered we had made reservations at the wrong hotel.

"How many Hiltons are there?"

"Apparently two," Heidi said. "That's what the guy told me. I must have made the reservations at the other one."

"Well, do they have room here?"

"I already got a double with a fold-out couch."

"I love you."

We parked the Penske and van in a far corner of the parking lot, because I was terrified of getting too close to other cars and not being able to maneuver in the morning. What I hadn't figured on was the damage that would be done by unloading our things from the van right next to the truck and then moving the truck in the dark "for better positioning." See, another one of my endearments is never leaving well enough alone. I have to take whatever works and, like the Beatles' Jude, make it better.

We discovered the squashed 35 mm camera and scattered articles of clothing in the morning. It was Heidi's camera. Pioneer woman that she is, she took it in stride and pulled out the Trip Tick itinerary and map for the day.

"We're driving to Salt Lake City today, which means going through the Salt Lake Desert. So the sooner we get there, the better."

others.

"Stopping in Elko for lunch?"

"Yes."

"Good. I'll need to refuel by then. Okay, girls, one last bathroom stop."

I made them go to the bathroom again, moaning all around, and then we hit the road. I shouldn't have had the stack of blueberry pancakes with an extra dollop of whipped butter, maple syrup, fried eggs, and bacon, because by Winnemucca I was comatose. I could barely keep my eyes open. Lena was riding with me and freaked out every time I jerked my head from dozing off. So, of course, I started doing it on purpose. We passed through Battle Mountain, Carlin, and into Elko, where we found a diner with a gas station. The diner had bulbous red booths with gold buttons and a thirty-page menu, each page as thick as a toddler's picture book. I liked eating in places like that, especially in Nevada, because they had slot machines that went ding-ding-ding, whistled, played xylophone music, and barked at you in carney voices to "Give it a whirl!" I think the girls liked it, too, since it was exotic and about as far from the plodding pace of the Village as you could get. We took up an entire booth, the five of us and Fred in his cage. I had suggested leaving him in the car, but the girls thought that was cruel.

We finished lunch. I paid the bill and gassed up the Penske, which had a fifty gallon tank and required a bank loan to fill, even with diesel. Then, naturally, I put a huge gash in the side pulling away from the pump, which was protected by a pair of concrete stanchions. They had come out of nowhere, I swear. It was like the Titanic ripping itself open on the iceberg, except it was hot as hell in Elko. I didn't get out or inspect the damage, but I could see Heidi holding her head as she sped ahead on I-80. We didn't stop again until the Bonneville Salt Flats, where it must have been about one hundred twenty degrees. Good thing we had taken the northern route. By then, I was completely paranoid about parked cars, turning space, and height limits. I had also mastered the fine art of using men's rooms without making direct physical contact with anything, which I was particularly proud of. You get a better appreciation of elbows and knees that way. Four hours later, we pulled into the Comfort Inn off Interstate 15 in Salt Lake City. I was completely drained, my foot was cramped from eight hours on the gas pedal, and I smelled more than ripe. I had also managed to park in a spot behind the hotel that only Houdini could get out of. Without Kenny, I was doomed. I decided to put it out of my mind and deal with it in the morning. We settled into our room, and then Deanna and I headed for the pool and Jacuzzi.

After dinner, we called "James" Okafor and made arrangements to meet him at the place he rented in Laramie. Since this was before the widespread use of cellphones—difficult as that may be to imagine, considering there are now more cellphones on the planet than people and may soon outnumber the total population of rats (city and country)—we had to do all of our communication via the hotel. So, calls to the dad in Laramie, my parents in New Jersey, and a friend or two of the girls in California had to be made in our room and added to the bill. If you've never placed a call from your room, believe me when I say it is neither cheap nor easy. You'd be much better off packing a spare cellphone charger. Of course, how many of those have I left in hotel rooms around the world? This may seem like a side note to the larger story, but dead cellphones are a metaphor, *mon ami*.

The next morning, our third on the road, we didn't get on the Interstate until 2:00 pm, partly because we had planned it that way, scheduling two short days of no more than five hundred miles. The drive from Salt Lake City to Laramie was four hundred, which should have been a piece of cake except for the other reason we got a late start: a complete breakdown of discipline. This was just what I had feared. I explained to the girls that they needed a set time to get up, do whatever it was they did in the bathroom (they each had fifteen minutes), and, on those days when we had a more flexible schedule, write postcards or buy souvenirs. As long as we were on the road at a reasonable hour, say, 10:00 am, noon at the latest, we would be all right. A 2:00 pm departure was unacceptable, especially since a trucker had taken pity on me and helped me maneuver out of the hotel parking lot. They listened in full agreement, nodded dutifully like good daughters, and then did whatever the hell they wanted. It also seemed that we were slowly losing things at each stop. At first it was hardly noticeable, but then, like a sinking cruise ship, you get up one morning, put your feet on the floor, and land in a puddle of ice-cold salt water. We had a serious leak. Whether it was a hairbrush, keychain, book, bracelet, hair tie, magazine, portable radio, or stuffed animal, it had to be replaced, which meant taking our caravan off the interstate to drive around shopping centers and malls for replacements. Driving a 22-foot Penske truck around malls was just about my worst nightmare. The only thing that made up for it was our stop at Little America off the Lincoln Highway. The giant penguin was still there. I was thrilled to death, but the girls just rolled their eyes, an expression they learned from their mother.

It took us six hours to reach the city limits of Laramie. By then, it was after eight o'clock and getting dark. By the time we found the street James lived on, Corthell Road, it was nighttime. He lived in a two-story house at the end of a long, paved driveway shared with other houses. So, the plan was to back the Penske up to the garage, avoiding the rain gutters of the other houses. Kenny was not there, but a few of the other kids were, so I relied on them and the girls for guidance. The problem was that Laramie has what I would call "reverse curbs." While most cities and towns in North America have a little stone or concrete edge for runoff, Laramie goes in the opposite direction with scooped-out depressions or dips. Backing up, you've got to make sure you have enough momentum to come up the other side of the dip or you'll be in trouble, especially with a heavy vehicle. Once I got behind the wheel and was ready to roll in reverse, I realized I had forgotten to check the depth of the dip.

"Girls, will I clear the dip with the truck?" I yelled out my window.

"What?"

"The little gully."

No response.

"The curb."

"Yes."

"Are you sure?"

"Go ahead."

So, I went ahead. The kids stood back, I revved the engine and put the transmission into reverse. The back of the truck dropped into the dip, rose up the other side, slid back down, swayed a bit, and then settled. I tried to pull out, going forward, but couldn't. Then I tried reverse again, but the weight of the furniture was too much. Leaving the final quarter of the truck for the Okafors meant that their heavy furniture was at the back, throwing the balance off and causing problems with handling. I had noticed it earlier driving around in search of scrunchies and sanitary pads.

"Just go forward, pull out of the dip, and give it all you've got in reverse," James said, running up to the truck. "You should have no problem."

I listened to him. After all, he was an anthropologist; he of all people should have known how to maneuver a Penske. I revved the engine and the truck jerked forward out of the dip. Then, after making sure everybody was safely away, I put it into reverse and floored the gas. The truck lurched backward and suddenly stopped, furniture crashing behind me.

"Uh, dad, I think you should look at this," Lena said, coming up to the cab.

"Look at what?"

"The pointy thing, it's stuck."

I stared at her.

"In the back."

I followed her to the back of the truck and looked at the pointy thing. As unbelievable as it sounds—I'm still not sure how it happened—when I revved the engine and the truck lurched backward, the trailer hitch, which had been at the level of the sidewalk because of the dip, plowed right through the concrete like a farmer's plow through clay. It was now embedded in the sidewalk. It was lodged so far in that the rear wheels of the truck were nearly halfway up the other side of the dip.

"All right, we'll have to unload the truck from here and carry the furniture down the driveway to the house."

"What about the truck?" Heidi asked.

"One thing at a time."

I unlocked the louvered door and furniture came crashing down around me.

"All right, troops, let's get moving!"

It took another hour to carry everything down the driveway to the garage. Some of the pieces had to be moved inside, like beds and couches, but for the most part it was relatively easy except for the fact that the driveway was about a hundred feet long and not well lit. It was more like an access road.

"Dad, it's late. I'm tired," Rose said.

"Keep working."

"I'm hungry," Deanna said.

"We'll eat as soon as we're done."

"Can I call Andrea?" Lena asked.

I looked at her.

When we finally finished, everyone took a ten-minute break and then reassembled at the truck to figure out how to extract it from the sidewalk. To say it was embarrassing is an understatement. Just as we were about to form committees, I jumped back into the driver's seat and revved the engine in second and third gears until the tires screeched and the engine smoked.

"Uh, I don't think it's working," Heidi said.

"Well, I can't just leave it here."

"What are we going to do?"

"I-I-I dunno."

Just then, James came over with a group of college students from across the street that had been partying and smelled the burning rubber.

"These guys have a jeep. They say they can pull you out of the dip," James said.

"Really?"

"Yes, sir," said one of them. "We've got chains and can hook them up to the front of your truck. Then we'll pull you out at the same time that you give it gas. That should do it."

I didn't like being called "sir."

"Sounds good," I said.

"Just don't ram us from behind with your truck."

"You got it."

I watched them back up their jeep, attach chains to both vehicles, and stagger around doing it. It made me recall my own drunken college days with fondness. What I wouldn't have given to be in college all over again. By then, a crowd of revelers had gathered on the open deck of the house where they had been partying. The deck overlooked the street and gave them a balcony-like view of the opera taking place on the street below. "Go, go, go…!" they chanted as the jeep started tugging and I revved the Penske. After more smoke and burning rubber, the trailer hitch broke free of the sidewalk, the truck leapt forward, and the crowd cheered, hooted, and hollered. We undid the chains, shook hands all around for a job well done, and went back to our respective sides of the street. The sidewalk was a mess, so I offered to reimburse James for whatever ticket or fine the city might impose.

"Don't worry," he said, smiling. "God will provide."

This would have been the end of the story, *should* have been the end, except for one little detail. It seems that the students, fumbling about in the dark, had attached the chains to the radiator instead of the truck's frame. So, when they pulled the truck out of the dip, they also pulled the radiator loose from its mounting. I hadn't noticed it until the next morning when I drove away from the Okafor house after a continental breakfast of fruit juice, brioche, and espresso. James and three of the kids had lined up outside like the Von Trapp family to wave goodbye. Deanna waved back from the truck. It was her turn to ride Uzi. She was excited about being my navigator and took out the map as soon as we turned the corner and headed for the interstate. We followed Heidi in the van through one traffic light, then another. She merged onto the interstate and we followed. Then something strange happened. Instead of speeding up, the Penske moaned, buckled, sputtered, and finally died. I was able to coast it to the side of the street away from traffic. The engine light came on and steam hissed from underneath the hood. We sat there in silence, watching Heidi's blue minivan disappear into the traffic of the interstate. We were stranded.

"Two days," the mechanic said.

We had been towed to the largest repair shop I have ever seen right at the interstate where all the truckers went to get their rigs fixed. You probably could have fit two football fields inside and still had room for a half-mile track. It was covered with a shiny aluminum roof that looked like it covered a village. Our Penske truck was a pipsqueak compared to the tractor trailers: the little Penske that couldn't.

"What?" I asked, trying to listen above the din of whirring, welding, shouting, and pneumatic drills.

"Two days. That's how long it will take to get the part."

"You don't have it here?"

"Well, normally we do but for some reason it's out of stock. We'll have to get it from Salt Lake City."

"Of course you will."

"What?"

"Nothing."

"We'll let you know was soon as it comes in."

"Thanks."

"You got a place to stay in Laramie?"

"I think so."

James was surprised to hear from us again, but he was cordial and offered his phone and car to go back and forth to the shop. For two days we sat around his house, had pleasant conversations about higher education and San Francisco, and went on long walks exploring Laramie. Well, I went on long walks. James had work to do and Deanna preferred to read or stay with the Okafor kids. I punctuated the routine with periodic calls to the shop and rental agency not out of any practical necessity but to assert myself in some way and not feel completely helpless, which, of course, I was. Heidi and I managed to get messages to each other through my parents in Jersey. We decided that instead of her turning back, she would keep driving and we would try to catch up with her at the Blackhawk Hotel in Davenport, Iowa. Our schedule had been thrown off, but the important thing was to get all of us back together.

"It's for you," James said, handing me the phone at the end of day two.

"I've got some bad news," the mechanic told me right off.

"What is it?"

"They sent us the wrong part."

"Wrong part?"

"That's right. We've got to order it again, but we're putting a rush on it."

"A rush."

"Yes."

"How long?"

"Well, these things usually take two days, but there's a possibility we'll get it by tomorrow morning."

I am not an unreasonable man. I know that things usually don't go smoothly right off the bat, out of the gate, day one. You expect to find a little wiggle room, a kink in the hose, a loose flange, an O-ring that doesn't quite fit, even a lug nut that wasn't tightened properly. But you never expect there to be one screw-up after another coming at you at the speed of Job. I may be mixing metaphors again, but I found myself dealing not just with the improbable but the incredible. After another series of phone calls to Jersey, trip recalculations with Heidi, and awkward reassurances from James that this new development was not a problem (I should have given them more room in the truck), I awoke the following morning to another phone call from the mechanic, whose name was Barry. I started referring to him as my case worker. The news wasn't what I had expected, to say the least. I thought he was going to say that they had fixed the truck and I could pick it up. Better yet, we're sending a limo for you with free champagne and deviled eggs. I like deviled eggs.

"I'm afraid I've got some bad news for you, Mister Branch-a-...Branch-a..."

This wasn't good. Anytime they revert to using my last name and butcher it like Stanley the Golden-Mouthed, I know I'm in trouble.

"Let me guess. Wrong part again?"

"No, it's not that. The part's here."

"So, what's the problem?"

"We're going to need some other parts."

"Other parts?"

"That's right."

"I don't understand."

"Well, uh, it seems that overnight a couple of our boys—you know, high school kids we hire to clean up the place and look after things—well, it seems some of them took a couple of the trucks and started racing around, playing chicken, doing wheelies inside the shop. You know, that sort of thing."

He paused. I didn't say anything, more amused than anything else.

"And, the truth of it is, your Penske was one of the trucks."

"One of the trucks?"

"Afraid so."

"They did wheelies with my truck with all the furniture inside?"

"Well, not exactly."

"Then what, *exactly*, did they do?"

"They played chicken."

"Chicken?"

"Smashed the driver's front end pretty bad, tore the bumper off, and crushed the fender. But we're working on it right now to get it running for you."

I looked at the receiver, then to James, Deanna, and the Okafor kids, all of whom were standing there waiting to hear the news.

"Barry?"

"Yes, sir."

"This is a joke, right? I mean, my wife put you up to this."

"No, sir."

"No?"

"Afraid not."

I paused. I could hear him waiting on the other end.

"All right, make sure Penske knows all about it and that I'm not charged a dime for any of the repairs."

"Oh, we already did that. There's nothing for you to worry about. They've authorized everything."

"Is there any damage to the furniture?"

"None as far as we can tell. A course, we didn't look inside or anything, but I don't believe so. Like I said, it was all done to the front end."

"So, when will it be ready?"

"We're doing our best to have everything done by closing time today."

"*Today?*"

"It's either today or Monday, cause tomorrow's Sunday and we're closed. But there's a good chance it'll be today."

I hung up and told everybody what had happened, but they just looked at me as if I had made it up, not that I blame them. It certainly sounded made up. I mean, why write fiction if your life is like this? On second thought, this is exactly why I write fiction. Then James brewed coffee, Deanna made waffles, and the Okafor kids reenacted the scene in the shop with miniature toys and trucks. Afterward, I related the story to my parents, who also thought I was making it up but eventually relayed the news to Heidi, who joined the rest of them in disbelief. She was at a Ramada Inn in Lincoln, Nebraska.

By 5:00 pm I hadn't heard anything, so I called Barry, who said to come over, they were just putting the finishing touches on the fender. Not exactly encouraging words (I pictured Moe, Larry, and Curly), but I was well aware that we had been at the Okafor's since Wednesday and that if we stayed any longer we'd have to pay rent. So, we said our goodbyes again, and James drove me and Deanna to the shop. He waited to make sure there weren't any other problems like the place burning down or a swarm of locust descending upon us. He had been good-natured about the whole thing, but I'm sure he was as anxious to get back to work as I was to get back on the road. I don't think either one of us could have survived another mishap.

"Dad, where are we going to spend the night?" Deanna asked once we were safely on the interstate.

"It's four hours to North Platte in Nebraska. I think we can make it. Besides, we've got to catch up to your mother."

"Four hours?"

"You'd rather stay in Laramie?"

"No."

The new Ford truck looked like crap. In addition to the gash in its side and the bent trailer hitch in the back, the front bumper was gone, making it look like a striped bass (not that I fish or anything). The fender was puttied and discolored, and the driver's headlight had been secured in place with, of all things, duct tape. If I hadn't been so depressed I would have laughed. Deanna settled down to her reading, and I breathed easier knowing that we were back on the road and making up for lost time.

One of the nice things about everything going wrong is that when you're done, you're done (theoretically, at least). If you've experienced nothing but misfortune, chances are you're home free, but the trick is not to do half measures. You have to experience all of the misfortune; otherwise there'll be more to come. In this case, there was. Suddenly, the sky turned black and there was a flash of lightening in the distance followed by an explosion of thunder. When they talk about rolling thunder, bowling balls and all, be assured that it really rolls, at least on the edge of the prairie. Deanna jumped, the truck swerved, and almost instantly we were in the middle of a thunderstorm with wind and rain whipping us in every direction. I slowed to about thirty-five but was determined to keep driving, fixing my eyes on the taillights about a hundred yards in front of me.

"Dad, shouldn't we stop?"

"No, never!"

"But I'm scared."

"Siempre adelante!"

"Dad!"

"All right."

I pulled onto the shoulder. Good thing, too, because the rain that had been coming down in biblical proportions suddenly turned to hail. I was beginning to think that if we didn't make it out alive, at least pharaoh's army would drown with us.

"Deanna, don't worry. As soon as it lets up, we'll find a motel off the interstate and spend the night there. We'll get a nice rest and an early start in the morning."

She looked at me.

"You like waffles, right? We'll go to a Waffle House for breakfast."

"They have a Waffle House here?"

"Sure they do. And don't worry. I've got everything under control."

"Okay, daddy."

Relieved, she sat back and doodled on the window, which was steamed up. The reality, of course, was that I had nothing under control, but kids don't want to hear that and probably shouldn't have to. Lies are good. They maintain the illusion of trust and stability so that the world can function. It's something I've learned over the years as a parent and human being. The truth is vastly overrated.

Another thing that is overrated, I'm sorry to say, is duct tape. For the most part, I've lived and died by duct tape, using it on everything from window screens to sunroofs. I used it on our VW bus when the gear mechanism got stuck, leaving a two-inch gap in the roof that exposed us to the elements. And I mean exposed. It made for great conversation in the winter when you'd stop at a red light and a wall of water would come cascading down from the roof to the floor behind you. So, I repaired it with duct tape, but the tape came undone on the freeway on our way to the Oakland airport the morning we were flying back East for Christmas. The tape flew off the roof because of more wind and rain, and within about three minutes the entire sunroof blew off the bus. It was like a hatch blowing on a lunar module. The roof smashed into a truck directly behind us, which, oddly enough, belonged to a roofing company filled with terrified undocumented workers. We arrived at the airport for our six-hour flight soaked and shivering. Uncle Frankie, who had driven us there, managed to retrieve the roof from Highway 101 on the way back. But I digress.

The hail stopped as quickly as it had begun, and so we got back on the road, trying to make up for more lost time. There were just a few cars on the interstate, the night sky had cleared, and I settled into a nice rhythm with an occasional thump-thump as the tires crossed an uneven patch of highway. It felt good to be moving again, and I was determined to catch up with Heidi in Davenport. But the duct tape had other ideas (backstage the band was falling apart?). The wind, rain, and hail had softened it so much that eventually it gave way just as it did on Highway 101. The left headlight, which up till then had been pointing a beam of light in a slightly skewed direction in front of us, as if the Penske were cross-eyed, now swung wildly back and forth by a thin electrical wire. I could see the highway in front of me on the upswing and the tall grass in the median on my left on the downswing. It came so unexpectedly—exploded, really—that I jumped, the truck swerved, furniture crashed in the compartment behind us, and Deanna woke with a scream.

"Daddy, what was that?"

"Just a technical malfunction. Don't worry, I have everything under control."

She looked at me, mouth open. She was doing a lot of that lately. I switched the cab light on, and she found a small town on the map east of Cheyenne that wasn't too far. Luckier still, it had a lot of street lights. Once there, we found a motel with a blinking neon sign announcing color TV. Each letter of "color" was in a different color. Clever, that. There was a dumpster in front with a couple of laundry carts next to it. Our room was clean, and there were even little friends lined up waiting for me in the minibar. It was the first break we had gotten in about four days. I drank all the liquor I could twist open—vodka, scotch, whiskey, something brown—and fell asleep in my clothes, too tired to make sure that my daughter was all right. It was only the second time in my life that I felt remiss in my duties as a father. I should probably qualify that by saying that I have failed a number of times, but this was only the second time I actually felt bad about it.

Let me interject here that if you are frustrated trying to figure out what any of this—funny though it may be—has to do with Bloomington, let me reassure you that we are coming up to that part of the story, which most people call the ending. My apologies for taking so long getting here, but, as you can see, this story needs plenty of baking and cooling (not that I bake or anything). The first thing I ought to do is provide an explanation about Bloomington. For instance, is it a high-end clothing store, an aircraft carrier, a member of the British royal family, a type of ladies' undergarment from the nineteenth century? No, it is none of these, although those are all good guesses and the reader ought to be given an "A" for effort, which is what students usually complain about. Since you are not my student, I won't go into my usual lecture about the outside world wanting results and not caring a rat's ass about how you got there. Consider it given.

"She wants to meet where?" I asked my mother the next morning from the room.

"Bloomington."

"But that's not a scheduled stop. We're supposed to meet in Davenport."

"I guess she got tired of waiting for you and they drove ahead."

"Tired of waiting for me?"

"I told you she's headstrong."

"But that puts more distance between us."

"Look, Robbie, I don't know what to tell you. She wants to meet you in Bloomington off Interstate Seventy-Four. She made a reservation at a Comfort Inn, only eighty-nine dollars for the night. Something about a pool and Jacuzzi. Right, Art, isn't that what she said?"

I could hear my father mumbling something in the background, papers shuffling, and then a lot of coughing.

"Yeah."

"So, there. Meet them in Bloomington. They're waiting for you."

We packed our things and got back on the road but had to stop shortly afterward at a truckers' diner for waffles. At first, Deanna was disappointed that there wasn't an actual Waffle House with a huge, yellow sign towering above the interstate, but she was a good kid with an even disposition, which probably wasn't easy to maintain in a house with three other females. She ordered two crispy waffles smeared with maple syrup, whipped butter, and two sizzling strips of bacon (it was before her vegan period). I had tea and toast, hold the butter. I wasn't taking any chances. We made it to Lincoln that night without incident except for pouring more cash into that drum of a gas tank. I swear, empty you could have played calypso music on it. I also secured the headlight with, you guessed it, more duct tape. We ended up staying at the same Ramada Inn near the airport where Heidi and the girls had stayed three nights earlier. The woman at the front desk remembered them.

"So, *you're* the husband with the other daughter," she said, gesturing toward Deanna, who stood there clutching a stuffed monkey.

"Well, for the life of me, ain't that a hoot. Yes, they were here all right. I remember them. Had a parakeet or something in a cage."

"That's them," I said, excited.

Suddenly, this woman with rhinestone glasses and blue hair was the thin electrical wire holding the two halves of our family together. And, since our family was swinging wildly to and fro, any piece of information or memory was a gift.

"Yep, the two girls got into some fight about a blouse. Made a ruckus. Their mother was embarrassed, I can tell you that."

I winced.

"Starting shoving each other right there where you're standing."

So much for sentimentality. But it only quickened my resolve to catch up to them so that we could be together for the triumphal downward stretch through Cincinnati and the Shenandoah Valley into Wheaton, Maryland. "Maryland" sounded so pleasant that I imagined its streets were paved with gold and that milk and honey gurgled up in its swampland. I was delirious. I would be even more delirious after the eight-hour day we were facing in the morning. So we said goodnight to the Blue Lady at the desk and went to our room.

"Don't worry, Deanna. By the end of the day tomorrow, we'll all be together again, I promise."

"Okay, daddy."

Note to self: I am always wrong. I'm not sure why that is, except maybe I am an eternal optimist who can't fathom how anything could ever not be what it ought to be, not at its core, anyway. I always expect the truth to prevail. But if you ever ask me anything, from the time of day to the top five draft picks in the NBA, don't listen to a word I say. It will be wrong. You can count on it. However—and this is a big however—there was that one time on the beach in Capitola when a woman on a blanket next to us asked if we had the time. Heidi told her no but I looked up at the sun, took some ridiculous measurements with my fingers, and said, "three-fifteen." Just then the woman's friend returned, so the woman asked her for the time. "Three-fifteen," the friend said, checking her watch. The woman looked back at me in astonishment.

"Oh, it's nothing. He does stuff like that all the time," Heidi said.

So, we drove and drove, past Omaha (didn't stop to say hello to Mr. Buffet), Des Moines, Davenport, and Peoria, where they rehearse the dance numbers before hitting Broadway. Finally, we arrived at Bloomington. Now, here's the thing: unbeknownst to me (and all concerned), there are two Bloomingtons just as there had been two Hiltons. *What did he say? Did I hear right?* Yes, you did. If you order now, we'll throw in a second set of Bloomington at no extra charge. That's right: two Bloomingtons for the price of one, but you have to act now! Call the number on your screen! To be more precise and for the purpose of this story, it is two cities, both nearly the same geographic size (22-24 square miles), with the same population at the time of our trip (65,000), although Bloomington, Illinois had more residents of German extraction according to the census. They were in neighboring states beginning with "I," and no more than one hundred seventy-five miles apart. There are only two things that distinguish them from each other: Bloomington, Indiana is the "Gateway to Scenic Southern Indiana" (as opposed to northern or eastern); Bloomington, Illinois is the home of State Farm Insurance's corporate headquarters. Apparently, when you need a good neighbor, you know where to go.

"Would you just tell her we're here when she calls?" I said to my mother after we arrived at the hotel in Bloomington, Illinois. "I don't understand why she isn't here to meet us."

"What did I tell you?"

"Mom, please."

"Fine."

"Are you at the Comfort Inn off Seventy?"

"I thought you said Seventy-Four"

"Okay, Seventy-Four."

"We're right in front where we said we'd meet."

"I'll tell her."

Having messages go back and forth through my parents was like trying to give instructions over the phone to a blind acupuncturist, but it was all we had. By 8:00 pm I called again from the hotel lobby.

"She wants to know where you are," my mother said.

"We're out front in a huge, yellow truck. You can't miss it."

"Well, she says it's not there."

"I'm pretty sure it is."

"Look, your father and I have to go to bed."

"Can you just stay up long enough to tell her to look for us?"

"Why don't you tell her yourself? Here's her number at the hotel."

"She already checked in?"

"Yeah, do you want the number?"

"Forget it. I'll just go to the front desk. Thanks!"

After some clicking on a computer terminal, double-checking paper files, and asking Amber of the Clueless Stare if "anybody from California checked in tonight," the clerk at the front desk, a nice enough guy in a blue blazer with a gold emblem, said, "I'm so sorry." He did it with such sincerity that I felt like I had just won a ribbon at the County Fair. You find that kind of thing only in the Midwest.

"All right, thanks."

I turned to leave but then stopped. I had a feeling.

"Is there another Comfort Inn?"

"Sir?"

"Another Comfort Inn here in Bloomington?"

"Well, yes, but it's clear across town."

"So this is the only one off Seventy-Four?"

"Yes, sir."

I turned away again as dejected as anybody could be, but then I thought of Deanna waiting outside with those big, brown eyes and decided to fight back. You know, not take it lying down anymore; grab the bull by the horns sort of thing. I went back to the clerk, who was beginning to look concerned for his safety.

"So, tell me, and—please—just humor me for a moment, would you?"

"Absolutely, sir."

I cleared my throat, leaned slightly across the desk, and smiled so as not to frighten the poor bastard.

"By any chance, any chance at all—" I said, spreading my arms in despair.

"Yes?"

"Is there *another* Bloomington?"

"Sir?"

"Another Bloomington, you know, like this one only *not* this one…Another one, another Bloomington…somewhere, anywhere?"

I waved my hand around in a circle as if to say that there might be another one right over there by the rack filled with State Farm and Aviation Air Museum brochures. You never know, what with physicists discovering multi-dimensions just about every other day. I must have looked like a madman.

He thought for a moment and said, "Well, not here in Illinois, but there is a Bloomington, Indiana."

"Ah-hah!" I yelled, slapping the desktop. "And do you happen to know if there is a Comfort Inn there?"

"Actually, there is."

"And is it also off Seventy-Four?"

"Well, no, but it's close to Interstate Seventy. In fact, you have to take Seventy to get there. Then it's a short drive on Thirty-Seven, I believe, just south of Indianapolis."

"How far from here?"

"Not far, maybe two hundred miles."

"Two hundred miles?"

"Yes, sir."

Even though this was the best news I had heard in days and I felt like Sherlock Holmes for figuring it all out, I didn't have the strength to go another two hundred feet, let alone two hundred miles. I knew Deanna was tired and hungry. Plus, there was no way I was maneuvering the Penske again. I also imagined my mother's reaction to all this: "Seventy-Four, Seventy, what do I know? Something with a seven. Maybe next time you can hire a secretary."

"Let me have a room, please."

"Two double beds?"

"That'll be fine."

I went back to the truck. Deanna was in the cab, which by then had become something of a pigsty, filled with empty milkshake cups (her favorite was strawberry), hamburger wrappers, straws, rubber bands, and barrettes. The heat was tapering off, although the simmering humidity and grime made you feel like your skin was made of puff paint.

"They're not here, are they?" she said, studying me as I approached the truck.

It broke my heart to have to admit it, but I shook my head.

"They're at another Comfort Inn in another Bloomington, but with any luck we'll catch up with them tomorrow."

She looked away, resigned to the reality of the situation. "Okay," she said.

I looked at my daughter. I can't be sure, but if I had to guess, I'd say that was the moment she became an adult, not that she welcomed the disappointment but that she accepted it as an inevitable part of living and, as such, something to be endured rather than fought. It was beautiful and profoundly sad at the same time.

"They have a pool here," I said. "Open till ten."

"That's nice."

The next morning, we ate breakfast at a Waffle House and caught up with Heidi and the girls that afternoon. There were hugs and smiles all around. I thought of the Americans meeting the Russians at the Elbe River in Germany. Deanna grabbed her things and locked herself in the van with her dirty monkey. It was Rose's turn to ride Uzi. She looked reluctant. The next two days were uneventful, comparatively speaking (not that that says a lot), but by the time we pulled up to the Penske rental office in Silver Spring after unloading our furniture, the truck was in ruins. I got out, slammed the door closed, and the engine bucked before dying in a last gasp of exhaust. Heidi sat outside on the curb, near tears. The amazing thing is that, because of the extra insurance I took out, not only did we not have to pay for any of the damages, but they gave us cash back. I didn't argue, ask questions, or wait for them to change their mind. Some things in life you just have to leave alone and not question. I exited the office with my best poker face. We jumped in the van and never looked back.

"God provides," I told Heidi.

"What?"

"Never mind. Let's go home."

Rocky the Friggin Squirrel

So there we were, sitting in the yard of our newly rented house in Maryland, enjoying the spring warmth after a harsh winter in which the town of Wheaton had all but shut down for two weeks in the worst snowstorm in a hundred years. I find that people say things like that whenever we're involved, but nevertheless it was true that the entire Washington, DC area was knee-deep in snow. Where there were drifts, it was waist deep. Many roads were closed and even the local Safeway had shut down. So we trudged to Mamma Lucia's on University Boulevard, the five of us, to warm ourselves with a hot lunch and listen to Papa Lucia play some Neapolitan ditties on his accordion. Afterward, we bought some supplies and mamma's homemade Italian bread right out of the oven. I remember stuffing the loaves down the front of our coats to keep the bread and our bodies warm. Then we marched back in single file through the snow as if it were a scene from *Doctor Zhivago*: me, Heidi, Lena, Rose, and Deanna. But now, as the song goes, those lonely days were over and we were enjoying the delicate warmth of a spring day in the Chesapeake Bay State. What could be better than that?

"Oh, would you look at that," Heidi said as she sat reading in the lounge chair in her broad-brimmed hat.

"What?"

"That squirrel eating the birdseed. Look at his little face and paws. How cute!"

I looked up at the bird feeder I had just hung from a branch in the elm tree that stood near the southwest corner of the house. Sure enough, there was a gray squirrel munching away feverishly and making a mess. There was definitely nothing cute about him. Heidi had picked up the feeder at a garage sale along with a picture frame on one of her strolls around the neighborhood. It had taken me hours to glue the loose pieces of the roof back together and insert the two glass sides that held the birdseed in place. What had taken so long was doing it in between trips to the grocery store, dropping one of the girls at a friend's, and figuring out the right kind of birdseed to attract birds in our area, which required research. It had also taken me a while to figure out how high up to place the feeder, which branch, how far out on the branch, and which side of the feeder to face the yard. What really got me, though, was that Heidi thought it was wonderful that this squirrel was the beneficiary of all that hard work.

"What's the problem?" she asked.

"No problem."

"Yes, there is. I can tell."

"It's a bird feeder, not a squirrel feeder," I said.

"Oh, I see."

I hated it when she said that.

"A little obsessive, are we?"

"Don't go social worker on me," I said, which was hard for her to do considering she was a social worker. I stuck out my tongue when she wasn't looking.

"I saw that."

She went back to her reading and lounging while I looked up at the squirrel and sulked. I got mad watching him ravage through the seed with abandon and even, yes, turning around every once in a while to snicker at me. Squirrels snicker, you know. It's a little known fact, but they do. This one had it out for me, even scattering birdseed my way as if to say, "Shit on you!" But I was having none of it. I decided right then and there not to let a squirrel make a monkey out of me, even if it took precious time away from the twenty-five page research paper I had to write on the "Anaphora of Addai and Mari," which is a Eucharistic prayer dating back to third-century Mesopotamia. I figured the Chaldean Church had survived this long without my invaluable insights; they could wait a little longer, just until I finished annihilating that goddamned rodent. Admittedly, my intentions weren't benign, but then territory is important. After all, isn't that what they are still fighting over in the Middle East? The truth is that I welcomed anything that might distract me from having to sit at my computer terminal by the window and watch spring float by like dandelion fluff. I was going to get rid of that squirrel no matter what. The fact that I started mumbling under my breath like Boris Badenov should have been a red flag. Unfortunately, like so many other times in my life when there were more red flags than a May Day parade in Beijing, it wasn't.

It began on a Saturday and didn't end till the following Wednesday. I won't ruin the story by telling you how it ends, but suffice it to say that by then I had only two days left to turn my paper in or risk another heart-to-heart talk with my advisor, who was "concerned" about my performance. If she hadn't been a Dominican nun, I would have told her not to worry about my performance, I hadn't had any complaints yet, which is a line from *A Night at The Opera*. Not that she would have thought it funny, but I would have, which is another problem. I've been making myself laugh all my life. I just wish other people had the same sense of humor. The nun didn't and neither did Heidi.[7]

---

[7] I once told another nun, an Ursuline, who was frustrated over how hard it was to get tickets to *Rent*, "Well, that's your problem right there," I said. "What?" "You have to

Heidi thought I was too fixated on the squirrel and not enough on getting us back to California, which was her and the girls' only objective from the moment we set foot in Wheaton. I don't blame them, really. They were California girls with only a theoretical understanding of winter and little appreciation for East Coast culture, customs, and language. They came from a place where the sun shone all the time and inventive types created things in the garage that revolutionized industries. The only thing in our garage was a bag of rock salt and half a can of wood lacquer left by the previous tenants.

Saturday consisted of me running out to the yard and chasing the squirrel away from the feeder every ten minutes. Finally, I threw sticks, which got him running—literally hightailing it—back up the tree trunk, across the roof of the house, and into the street, where I hoped he would get flattened by a passing car or delivery truck, but no such luck. Sunday came and, except for those times when we were away from the house—church, shopping at the Wheaton mall, more neighborhood walks, I began storing sticks and old shoes so that I would be ready in case of a sneak attack by the varmint, which apparently had gotten the idea that its mission in life was to eat as much birdseed as possible while giving me the middle claw. In fact, I wasn't sure at all whether he was doing it because he was hungry or just to piss me off. I mean, really, how much birdseed could a squirrel eat?

"How much wood would a woodchuck chuck if a woodchuck could chuck wood?" Heidi said, smirking.

"Very funny, but I'm going to get that squirrel if it's the last thing I do."

"That's my man."

---

buy them." I am thinking of putting a collection of nun stories together. I will call it *Nun Sense*.

I started thinking of more inventive ways of getting rid of "Rocky." For instance, I noticed that if he saw me watching and waiting, even though I stood behind the large windows of our sun porch, he wouldn't come out. So I started hiding and sneaking up on him, sticks flying. He would scamper away but always return. So I got the ladder and moved the feeder out farther onto the branch, since the squirrel had been jumping from the tree trunk to the feeder like some sort of Chinese acrobat. Moving the feeder away from the trunk would solve that problem, or so I thought. Rocky sized up the situation, figured out that the feeder was too far, and simply went out on the tree limb and down the rope to the feeder. This was even easier for him, since it didn't involve leaping. By Sunday night, I thought I had solved this problem by lowering the feeder so that it hung a good two-and-a-half feet from the limb, which I thought would make Rocky more vulnerable to attack. Either he would be a sitting duck, so to speak, or he would see the futility of the situation and find some other birdfeeder to pillage. I was trying to be reasonable, since, as I have stated, I am a reasonable man.

Wrong again. Monday morning after the kids had gone to school and Heidi to work, I found him sitting there munching away without a care in the world, which, even at 9:00 am enraged me so much that I took to throwing kitchen knives instead of sticks. This was now all out war. I really wanted to kill him and stretch his carcass over a lampshade in the living room, but I knew the girls would get upset. So I decided to stick to deterrence; that is, to prevent the rabid, infectious mammal from getting to the feeder. I knew that if I constructed something to block his way down the rope, he would be unable to get to the birdseed and eventually give up. That was the theory. But what could I use? I settled on a plastic garbage can cover only because it was handy. I lowered the feeder to put the cover in place. I cut a hole in the center of the cover, slipped the rope through, retied the rope to the feeder, and hoisted it like a flag back up the tree limb. That's when I ran into another technical problem: balance. The plastic cover needed to be weighted in such a way that it remained perpendicular to the rope, thus preventing Rocky from climbing around it. Otherwise, he would be able to stay on the rope, bypass the cover, and get to the feeder. So, I used—what else?—duct tape to hang various fishing weights around the cover to balance it. The fishing weights had also been handy. When finished, it held its shape but looked like a plastic flamenco hat with lead, fishing tassels. Rocky must have sensed something was up, because I spent all afternoon waiting for him, but he never showed his little, rat face.

"Have a productive day?" Heidi asked when she got home that evening.

"Uh, yeah."

"You going back to work then?"

"No, I'm still not done."

"So how's it going?"

"Oh, you know, fine."

"That's good."

"Dad, can you help me with my algebra?" Rose asked.

"Sure, just let me check something first."

I snuck out to the yard, peered around the corner of the house, and saw him sitting there, perched on the feeder, fattening himself on the birdseed that Heidi bought with the money she earned from talking to crazy people at Providence Hospital. I yelled, threw whatever I could get my hands on, and shook my fists like a wild man. If I could have, I would have squeezed him into a compact ball of bone, blood, and fur with my bare fingers. Then, maybe Heidi would be talking to me at Providence Hospital in addition to her other patients. It didn't matter. Was it my imagination, or was he taking longer and longer to run away? I swear his rump was even bigger. Then I looked back and saw Heidi, Lena, Rose, and Deanna staring at me from the sun porch. I didn't say anything and went back inside.

One of the things that you take away from reading Caesar's *Commentaries on the Gallic War* is that an overwhelming force, while a significant factor in battle, may not be the deciding factor. As impressive as a large army might be, what wins wars are cunning and ingenuity. Caesar defeated a quarter million tribesmen on the field at Alesia in Gaul with only forty thousand legionaries through deceptive strategy. Of course, planting a minefield didn't hurt; neither did four hundred, cyborg-like, German cavalry who enjoyed cutting down their neighbors even more than they hated the Romans. The Gauls didn't have that cool Roman *sobrietas* running through their veins like ice water. They also didn't have engineering, which is what enabled the Romans to conquer everything from Scotland to the Caspian Sea and the Straits of Gibraltar to Luxor. The Romans built siege machines, erected towers, excavated mines, redirected streams, built bridges, tore those same bridges down when they were done with them, set elaborate traps, fired blazing rockets with catapults, and generally out bad-assed the bad asses. This one insight gave me a distinct advantage over Rocky besides my numerical superiority, which consisted of my height, not the number of ground troops. I was also pretty sure that the squirrel had not read the *Commentaries*, and so, smug as a bug in a rug, I went to work to fix the rascal for good. And I mean good. *Requiescat in pace, o Roce!*

"So, you've got a squirrel problem?" the guy at the local hardware store asked the next morning as I showed up bright and early after Heidi and the girls had left the house.

"That's right."

"What's going on?"

"It's eating our birdseed."

"Just one?"

I nodded.

"Why don't you shoot the thing and be done with it? My cousin Elmer shoots them all the time with his twenty-two and then eats them."

"You have a cousin Elmer?"

"Yep."

"He eats squirrels?"

"Cooks 'em first."

"I see."

"You could try that."

"You sell guns here?"

"No, you've got to go to a gun shop for that."

I hadn't thought about shooting Rocky. I liked the idea, but it seemed extreme. I decided to do it only as a last resort.

"I'll hold off on that for the time being."

"Suit yourself."

"So, let me have a quart of power steering fluid, a can of Drano, a pair of snow chains, and a flare."

I was starting to sound like Bill Murray. Oddly enough, as the guy rang it all up, I didn't consider any of that extreme. Yes, this was total war, but I would look pretty silly if I went around with a flamethrower or even a .22 rifle to kill the thing, not that I hadn't fantasized about it, including taking target practice on old soda cans in the woods near our house. But why drop the equivalent of an H-bomb when I could just as easily do the job with Drano? I would conduct total war in the most efficient manner possible, expending as little energy as possible. That's what the Roman did. I had already wasted three full days on Rocky and had accomplished nothing. I had done nothing on my paper except stack books by the computer in a nice little pile, which somehow made me feel better. All I needed to get back to work on that third-century Eucharistic prayer was the fluffy pelt of a major pain in the ass. I'd go to confession afterward.

I rushed back home and went to work. I took the feeder down and spread wood glue over the top, sprinkling it with a generous dose of Drano. Then I ran the portion of the rope above the garbage can cover through the snow chains so that the chains formed a loose net that I figured would either trap the squirrel or prevent him from landing on the cover below. I poured power steering fluid on the snow chains, rope, and cover. Then I hoisted everything back up on the tree, tied it off, and stood back. There was the bird feeder with Drano glued to the roof, the rope glistening with red power steering fluid, the garbage can cover with fishing weights dangling from its lip, and the snow chains looking like a crab net. I stepped back farther to see if any of it made sense. I wasn't sure, but it certainly was a contraption Rube Goldberg would have been proud of. I just hoped it worked. If it didn't, I still had the flare, which I would use like a flamethrower. Combined with the power steering fluid, it was sure to do the job. You have to have a Plan B.

I waited. I waited all day. I waited all day but nothing happened except for me getting antsy. No squirrel, no birds, no writing about Addai and Mari, not even the man walking his nearly blind German Shepherd every day at the same time, 1:00 pm, on the path beside our house on Alberti Drive that led to Glen Haven Elementary School just beyond our yard. In a word, nothing. Rocky was toying with me. I didn't know what to do with myself. If he didn't show up soon, I would be left to face the absurd reality that I had now wasted four days on a squirrel. I would have to go back to the paper, back to work, back to being a level-headed dad with duties and responsibilities and an adult life to lead.

Where was that squirrel?

"What did you say?" Heidi asked.

She had come home early, the girls' practice was over, and we decided to eat a light dinner on the sun porch overlooking the yard.

"Nothing, I didn't say anything."

"I thought you did."

"Dad, are you all right?" Lena asked.

"Couldn't be better. Why do you ask?"

"You're acting a little...strange."

I looked at her. Lena, a fireplug of a girl with a dynamo personality that attracted everyone to her, had been through everything with us. I'm not sure how she did it, but at five feet, two inches, she even managed to get on the Albert Einstein High School volleyball team.

"No, really, I'm fine. I just have a lot on my mind, that's all. Your old dad's just fine. So, how was squirrel today?"

"*Squirrel?*"

"School!"

Lena looked at her mom, who looked at Rose, who looked at Deanna, who looked at me with those brown eyes. Then they all turned to the window closest to the elm tree. There it was in all its glory: my toxin-laced, garbage can-covered, red glistening bird feeder with the squirrel munching away at the birdseed as if nothing had happened. It didn't have a care in the world. It was like watching the Titanic go down.

"Dad, what is that?" Rose asked.

"What is what?"

"That," she said, pointing.

"Oh, it's just the birdfeeder."

"What did you do to it?"

"I made some adjustments...for Rocky."

"Rocky?" Heidi said. "You named it?"

"Yeah, you know, Rocky the friggin squirrel."

Nearly crying, I dug into my potato salad and took a long gulp of white zinfandel. Then, as I put the glass down, something happened. I don't know what it was—maybe the crying, maybe the zinfandel—but I snapped. I grabbed my steak knife and walked quietly out to the yard. This time, I caught the sonofabitch off guard. He scrambled up the rope, slipped trying to climb through the power steering fluid, and made a tactical mistake by jumping to the tree trunk. I thought I had him and chased him around the trunk. That's when something else happened, something amazing. It seems that the escape route over the roof and into the front yard was just a subterfuge, a ruse, because after the dust settled, Rocky would double-back to the yard next door, where he had a burrow or nest with his mate. How do I know this? Because just then the mate came scurrying out from the neighbor's yard and started chittering-chattering-sputtering-woodchuck-chucking at me. It came within ten feet and stopped, making all kinds of noises and twirling like a dervish. I decided that a bird in the hand was worth two in the bush and went after it. But it dodged my knife and scampered away to its burrow, giving Rocky a chance to escape up the tree and across the roof to safety.

"Did you see that?" I yelled up at the sun porch where the four of them were crammed at the screen, watching me.

"Oh we saw it, all right," Heidi said.

"That one acted like a decoy so Rocky could escape."

"Uh huh."

"They were working together."

"Right."

I looked back and forth from the sun porch to the feeder and finally went inside. Hemingway was wrong after all. A man can be destroyed as well as defeated. I felt like the old man in *The Old Man and the Sea*.

"You know, I've been thinking about buying a twenty-two rifle," I said some time later. "I think you girls would love it. We could take target practice in the woods. What do you say to that?"

"We love you, dad," they said.

Red Dogs, Blue Trees

I don't have a lot of possessions. I've never felt the need for them, although I appreciate chrome and would not turn down a 1958 Chrysler Imperial convertible if offered one. So even though I lead a monastic life, I am not Mother Teresa, which you already knew. In fact, there are certain things that I cannot do without like my metal, insurance file cabinet and cashmere overcoat. But, truthfully, I am more interested in a finely-balanced London dry gin than a Poltrone love seat, a dark espresso in the morning than a sterling spoon to stir it with (although that is exactly what I stir it with). I also own a piano, a Kawai console made of polished cherry wood. Up until I bought it, I had assumed Kawai was one of the Hawaiian islands, but the salesman set me straight about that. I bought it one day on a whim as I walked along Lafayette Street behind Santa Clara University, minding my own business. I get into more trouble that way. It was one of those pleasant spring days that occur only in a place like Santa Clara: clear, sunny, seventy-five degrees, slight wind out of the northwest. That's pretty much the weather every day of the year in the Bay Area. With weather like that, you'd think there'd be no crime, but there is. Unfortunately, people have a nasty habit of finding something to fight about even in paradise. Anyway, on this spring day filled with sunshine and chirping, I passed a sign that said, "Big Piano Sale."

I didn't need a big piano. I didn't even need a small one, but I wanted one. I had wanted one for the longest time, ever since watching *White Christmas* with Bing Crosby and Danny Kaye. I used to marvel at how they could whip up a tune from out of nowhere and then sit down at the piano and play as if they had been taking lessons all their lives. I, too, wanted to gather the gang around a piano and pound out show tunes and rousing drinking songs that lasted for hours. I remember this one from college:

> R. I used to work in Chicago
> in a department store,
> I used to work in Chicago
> but I'll never work there anymore.
>
> A lady came in for a hat one day.
> I asked her what kind she wished.
> 'Felt,' she said.
> So, felt her I did.
> I'll never work there anymore.
>
> I used to work in Chicago…

This piano thing, this itch, had been working its way into my limbic system for years with every holiday, birthday party, dinner at a piano bar, and shopping trip to Nordstrom's where I would position myself strategically to listen to the piano while I waited like a dutiful husband/father/friend/ retiree/slave/golden retriever for the shopping to end. The pianist would usually be some college kid dressed in an ill-fitting, rented tuxedo with unkempt hair and an intense expression as if to tell everyone that even though this was a department store and people were gabbing and yelling and getting lost all around him, it was still a Debussy piano étude, goddamn it, and he would play it the way it was meant to be played. He would become absorbed in the music until they interrupted with some annoying announcement about the latest "amazing" discount on junior miss sportswear. Life is like that: red pushpins of beauty sticking out on a map of the mundane and stupid. But it shouldn't be like that. It should be the other way around. You should be able to go to Nordstrom's to hear Debussy and every once in a while wander over to the Junior Miss department or Men's Raincoats to see what's going on. Is there such a thing as Men's Raincoats? I don't know, but I would probably wander over to find out just for the sake of walking. Do they serve espresso?

On that spring day, I made the turn toward the Music Department at the university to see what was going on. That's where the sale was happening. I can't say it was a decision, because I really didn't decide anything and could just as easily have continued walking, which is what I've done every other time I had an opportunity like this. I have a fear of spending money (*pecuniae impendere metu*), which was even stronger than my desire to be Danny Kaye. Still, I figured what harm could there be in having a look? It was the Music Department, so it wasn't as if they were going to swarm around me the way they do at a car dealership, right? So, I went inside to kick a few tires, poke under the hood, and play a little boogie-woogie on the keyboard. At least, that's what I told the salesman, and he was a salesman. I guess I was expecting a bespectacled, professorial type with a goatee and tweed, but this guy was straight from the piano dealer and had one thing on his mind (not études). Three hours later, I left with a piano. Well, I had a fancy receipt and a "World of Kawai" brochure. They delivered the piano the following week.

Now that I owned a piano, I figured I should probably learn how to play it. So I went to Barnes and Noble to buy a book on how to play the piano. I still remember the name of the book: *How to Play the Piano*. It was about sixty pages long and had drawings that showed you how to sit, how to hold your hands, how far the piano should be from the wall, how to play scales, and about four or five songs at the end to make you feel like you accomplished something. Uncharacteristically, I started at the beginning. By the time I got to *Waltzing Matilda* at the end, I was ecstatic and ready to invite my friends and family over for my debut performance. Before that, though, I wanted to practice in front of a live audience, since the book said that it was important to get used to playing with people in the room so you wouldn't vomit during a real performance. Audiences tend to look down on that sort of thing, especially the ones in the front row. Up till then, I had played only when I was alone and wouldn't even do it when the cable guy or plumber was in the room. So, I had Lena and Rose over along with my granddaughter, Daniella, who was three-and-a-half at the time (forty-two months).

I need to tell you something about Daniella Brancatella, Lena's daughter, who was a pill even then. She had light red hair (orange, really), bright hazel eyes, and a stubborn streak that must have come from my ex-wife's side of the family. Honestly, between her Sicilian and Austrian blood, the poor kid didn't stand a chance. Or, more to the point, the rest of us didn't stand a chance. Not only was there stubbornness on both sides, but red hair as well. That was a deadly combination for anyone to have, let alone an incredibly disarming, little girl with a fifth-grade vocabulary. I called her Daniella Brancatella only partly to rhyme her name and annoy her. I also did it because our name truthfully and rightfully ends in "a," not "i." The story goes that when my grandmother registered my father for kindergarten, she decided to change the ending even though his birth certificate clearly stated, "Arthur Anthony Brancatella."[8]

---

[8] This caused enough of a problem for my father that, as a young man working for Boeing Corporation in Texas, the FBI paid him a visit to inquire about the name change. That was in

Apparently, Italians of that generation did that a lot: changed names to suit their tastes, or because the new name reflected a higher social status (i.e., "i" indicates someone from the tech-savvy North, "a" from the feudal South). In any case, they either did it or let it happen, because accurate recordkeeping didn't mean a lot to them, unless there was an advantage in it somehow. When we named Lena, we thought it was after my grandmother on my mother's side. Turns out that even though they called my grandmother Lena, her name was Nina, which was short for Antonina, her real name. So, in essence, I got that wrong, too. Only Italians have nicknames for nicknames.

At the time, I was living in a two-bedroom apartment in faculty housing. Heidi and I had just divorced, and I was living paycheck-to-paycheck without any furniture. I had a ceramic bowl made by Deanna when she was in grade school, a bent fork and spoon, and a futon mattress without the frame but with a sleeping bag that I had used years earlier during my post-graduation trek across North America in a pair of hiking boots. I also had a black, rotary phone made of Bakelite that I had salvaged from a storeroom in the old St. Joseph Seminary in Los Altos Hills, which came down in the 1989 Loma Prieta earthquake. I had it "modularized" at the AT&T store, and it worked beautifully. Eventually, I bought a cherry wood dining table from Breuner's for pennies on the dollar, because there were scratches on the surface, which I easily buffed out. I loved the table and thought it lent my paltry living room a certain charm. It reminded me of the time I interviewed with the provost of a college in New Orleans (pre-diluvium). The woman wore a pleated, wool skirt and, leaning against a cherry

---

1957. In hindsight, they would have been better off doing a more thorough investigation of Lee Harvey Oswald, but that's water under the overpass.

wood credenza with her arms crossed, asked me why I thought I was the better candidate for the position. She was wasting her time, though, because I had already decided it wasn't the right job for me ever since discovering earlier that day that it wasn't fog I was breathing but steam. I wondered why it rose up from the ground instead of floated in off the ocean (that's what living in the Bay Area will do to you). I told her I had no idea if I was the better candidate; I hadn't met the other guy. That appeared to stun her. I didn't get the job, which didn't stun me. I'd rather live in a place where I can breathe and there are no poisonous snakes.

I don't know much about Obsessive Compulsive Disorder (OCD), not clinically, at least, but then you don't need a public health degree to know that it affects a lot of people and is an awful condition. It robs you of energy, money, friends, and even your job. Worse, it robs you of time, which is the most precious thing in existence. I can't tell you how much time I've wasted going through daily rituals like making coffee with a certain level of water in the pot (cold, from the tap— none of that snooty bottled H20 for me), studying in the most laborious way possible (do I really need to read Heidegger in German to learn the language?), and following a routine like showering, shaving, ironing, and taking out the garbage with meticulous precision. Yes, you can take out the garbage with meticulous precision. It takes practice, of course.

I have OCD, that's a fact, but I hide it well. Not well enough, mind you, to avoid being caught by a student once during Mass folding the church bulletin in sharp, even creases so that the corners fit perfectly. In my own defense, the quality of the homily may have had something to do with it, not to mention the carelessness of the original folding job. Order is important, but the right order is even more important, because it is not enough to have order. If you have order that is out of order, then you're asking for trouble, because you will never be ready for anything. I am notorious for getting up at 3:00 am for an 8:30 flight and being late to the airport (without my wallet). There are things that must get done prior to traveling for the day, and just because it's a travel day doesn't mean you can go off schedule and do whatever the hell pleases you. What would happen then? You might as well stay in bed all day, smoking cigarettes and eating Graham crackers (not that I've done that, you understand).

"Dad, we don't have enough chairs," Rose said, arranging the table for dinner on the night of my practice performance.

It was to be dinner and a show. The "show" consisted of my playing *Red River Valley, Waltzing Matilda*, and *O Holy Night* on the Kawai. It was July, not Christmas, but this was a special performance for select people. Some disorder you have to accept in life. Besides, when I got to *O Holy Night*, I figured the girls would have Celine Dion on their minds and not notice how much their old man botched the music.

"I'll move the piano bench over and Daniella and I can sit on that."

I set the cherry wood, piano bench at the table and went into the kitchen to help Lena with the eggplant and salad. In this family, we're big on Caesar salad and eggplant parmigiana. Add fresh bread and a nice *vino da tavola*, and you've got yourself a meal. Plus, Lena has a gift for whipping up incredible dishes on the spur of the moment, almost magically. The fact that she had time to plan this one made it even better, although I think she does her best work under pressure. I suppose that makes her a pressure cooker. I am not sure what that says about the artistic process, but I am convinced that thinking too much destroys inspiration. That's why I have always been wary of artists who go on and on about the meaning of art. Really, who cares? Instead of theorizing about it, why don't you just do it? In my mind, it's like people who talk excessively about sex. They're the ones who never roll up their sleeves, as it were, and dive in. I was thinking of all this when I noticed that the bench was back at the piano.

Now, I can be a little forgetful, sometimes absent-minded, occasionally delusional, depending on which ex-wife/girlfriend/friend you ask, so I thought maybe I had imagined moving the bench but hadn't actually done so. I've done things like that before, mainly over minor details like whether or not I've brushed my teeth or zippered my fly, which may not be so minor in certain circumstances, said circumstances related to how close the listener is. I've figured out that all I have to do is see if the toothbrush is still wet or I feel a draft. See, there's an answer for everything. I've also gotten into the habit of checking and rechecking my zipper, but that poses other problems, especially standing in front of a room of college students. So I moved the bench back to the table and went about my business. Not long afterward, I noticed that it had returned yet again to the piano.

"All right, who's makin a monkey outta me?"

I surveyed the room, which contained the dining table, piano, a small couch given to me by my brother, and a bookcase held together with (you guessed it) duct tape. Rose had gone to the bathroom and Daniella was in a corner with her nose in a book. The book was my favorite as a kid and one that I had begun reading to her: *Go, Dog. Go!* I even enjoyed it as an adult, since I like to wear hats of all kinds and go around at parties asking people, "Do you like my hat?" Whenever I asked Daniella, she would answer, "I do not like it" and giggle. I looked over at her again. She seemed to be looking back at me without actually looking, as if she were aware of my presence but did not want to engage. If I didn't know any better, I'd say she was hiding something, but what? Was she capable of doing something on the sly and then covering it up? How does a child of forty-two months do that? She was such a sweet, little girl. I felt guilty for even thinking it. Still, I thought of the genes, the red hair, the precociousness, the stories my mother told of me at that age.

Being a reasonable man, as noted, I decided that the situation called for rational inquiry, and the first step in rational inquiry is to collect the facts. What did I know? I knew that I definitely moved the piano bench to the dining table. That was not an illusion but a fact. Furthermore, I had moved it not once but twice. I also knew that whenever I turned away, it somehow made its way back to the piano. Based on a combination of fact and extrapolation, I also knew that a piano bench could not just get up and walk around on its own, which meant that the effect of its being back at the piano was the result of some cause external to itself. That cause had to be intelligent, willful, and conscious. See what a Jesuit education will do for you? I was definitely getting places. Now, who was in the immediate vicinity that met all those conditions? I looked at Daniella, who was engaged intently in reading, or so it appeared. There was no one else in the room, no one else in the entire apartment unaccounted for, and, although the windows were open, there was no way anybody could have entered without my knowledge and moved the bench. Even if that were the case, why in God's name would anyone want to do that? Wouldn't they just ring the doorbell, wait to be invited to dinner, and then move the bench under everyone's smiling gaze? That raised another dimension of the piano bench riddle that I hadn't even considered but that was perhaps the most intriguing. It is the great philosophical question in all inquiry of piano benches. *Why* had it been moved?

Again, I looked at Daniella Brancatella, the little, redheaded girl in curls. There was obviously more going on there than met the eye, so I decided to do some investigative work. I sat down in the corner next to her and waited. She did not look up but instead kept reading, turning the pages slowly.

I'm not so convinced she was reading as much as making up stories to accompany the pictures. She may have recognized a coordinate conjunction here and there like "and" or "but," but otherwise she was on her own, flying by the seat of her imagination, which I had a great deal of respect for. It took a lot of guts to create a story from scratch in a world that was new to you and where everyone towered above you. I wouldn't have wanted to be in her kiddie shoes, sophisticated though they were.

"So, Daniella, do you like the book?"

"Oh, yes," she said, nodding.

"Why?"

"All the doggies."

"You like them?"

She paused for a moment and said, "Yes, but not all the time."

"Really? When don't you like them?"

"When they do things they shouldn't do."

"I see. So, when does that happen?"

This was a tough one. She started to answer, got flustered, and gave up.

"Can you show me?"

She opened to a page in the book. "See?"

"I don't understand."

She pointed to the left side of the page where there was a dog in a tree. To be more specific, it was a red dog in a blue tree.

"The dog is red, but the tree is blue," she said.

"Okay."

Then she pointed to the drawing just below it with a blue dog in a red tree. She put her forefinger on the tree.

"The blue doggie is in a red tree."

"Right."

She stopped, smoothed the page with her little hand, and looked up at me, hoping that I would make sense out of the chaos that was so unnerving she couldn't even bring up the third illustration, which—*me miserum!*—was a green dog in a yellow tree. It was as if all hell had broken loose.

"So, the problem is the red dog in the blue tree and the blue dog in the red tree, right?" I said.

She nodded and flipped ahead to a page where all the dogs were asleep in a big bed. They were all the same color in the dark. She took a sigh of relief.

"Gotta keep the red dogs in the red trees and the blue dogs in the blue trees," I said.

"Uh huh."

"Got it."

I left her to her reading, amazed at her drive—all right, let's call it what it is, obsession—to maintain strict order and form. She definitely had *sobrietas* going for her. Unfortunately, the real world tends toward chaos, which I figured would be a conversation for some other time, maybe the third grade. Meanwhile, we needed the bench for dinner, so I moved it to the table and went into the kitchen, hoping that, at least for the time being, pianos and their benches might be separated from each other without tearing a hole in the fabric of the universe. I envisioned it as a kind of Sabbath for piano atoms.

By now, Lena had caught on that something was up, and Rose had come out of the bathroom. The three of us watched from the kitchen as Daniella put the book down, checked to see if anyone was watching, and ran over to the piano bench. It was bigger than her, but she managed to drag it back to the piano, centering it carefully under the keyboard. One has to be thorough in these things. Otherwise, what's the point? Then she settled all snug in the corner as if nothing had happened. That's when I noticed the telltale streaks on the carpet as if a body had been dragged off to sleep with the fishes.

Odd, but I hadn't noticed them before. So maybe a Sherlock I am not.

"Okay, so what's going on?" Lena asked.

"A little genetic OCD," I said. "Reminds me of a squirrel and a bird feeder."

"Great, dad."

"It's your mother's fault."

"How do you know it's OCD?" Rose asked.

"Follow me."

I led them into the living room where we went up to Daniella, who pretended to be reading. "Daniella, did you move the piano bench back to the piano?"

She nodded without looking up.

"Tell your mommy and tante why."

She tried to explain, got flustered again, and looked at me for help.

"Go ahead, it's all right."

"Red dogs, blue trees," she said. Then she went back to her reading as if this needed no further explanation.

"Well, there you have it," I told my daughters.

"Have what?" Lena asked.

"Why you can't argue with OCD, at least not logically."

"But dad—"

"We can use the plastic chairs from the patio."

And that's how we ate dinner: two folding, wooden chairs and two plastic chairs. We had to put the folding chairs on one side of the table and the plastic chairs on the other to maintain the proper balance, but it was a small price to pay to see Daniella at peace. There's too much anxiety in our family as it is, what with people torturing themselves over all kinds of things: finding a job, finding themselves, finding their keys, moving furniture, getting to school on time, getting sick, getting old, not being old enough, getting that bump in the nose fixed, losing weight, cleaning the dirt that has accumulated in the cracks of the wooden floor, waxing the pickup that nobody ever drives, checking and rechecking zippers, making sure the stove is turned off and the iron unplugged, releasing the hand brake until it nearly breaks, putting the toiletries in order on the bathroom windowsill, brushing so hard that the enamel wears off your teeth, and arranging books in the bookcase alphabetically by subject area, author last name, and size. Try that one.

Frankly, it's exhausting, and I wonder what we might be capable of if we cut the time we obsess over things by half. That might be too much to ask. Is it even possible to do, especially if we're fighting the genetic code? How about if we set our goal at twenty-five percent? Fifteen? We might invent a self-renewable energy source that would relieve our nation's dependence on oil and coal. Or figure out the family curse. Learn typing. Trap squirrels. I could learn *Waltzing Matilda* by heart. Right now, though, we're preoccupied with the problem of red dogs in blue trees. I suppose you've got to start small and work your way up.

Misery, the Mother

of Intention

I've read a million articles, maybe a million-and-a-half, about the secret to success, whether in business, politics, law, medicine, entertainment, running a bagel factory, or sex. The secret, so it seems, is persistence, as in never giving up. That's probably why pharmaceutical companies are in the stamina business. Don't give up, because bouncing back from failure is what success is all about and separates the men from the boys, the sheep from the goats, winners from losers, up from down, etc. These articles describe Larry Page, Richard Branson, Oprah Winfrey, and a host of other entrepreneurs who kept at their invention or dream until it came true. Thomas Edison famously declared that he never failed at anything; he just discovered ten thousand ways how *not* to make a light bulb before finding one that worked. I knew a pastor who believed in this principle so much that he put a huge banner out front of his church that said "Never Give Up!" It was perfect at Easter, because in his homilies he would explain how Jesus never gave up and was able to bounce back against all odds, even death, "So you can, too!" It sounded bizarre, as if Jesus had just botched a field goal or given a bad job interview. Maybe he didn't know you're not supposed to bring up salary or benefits. Don't worry, dude, you'll nail it next time! Well, in a manner of speaking.

The Brancatellis have taken this advice to heart. Sure, we know that talent, timing, and a little secret sauce are also needed to be successful, but we have clung onto persistence as the one factor that will make or break you. Whether we do it because we are genuinely convinced of its importance or simply stubborn, it still works to our advantage, because we come up with a bright idea every twenty minutes. But bright ideas are a dime a dozen, even after inflation, which means that if we are not persistent, we'll get nowhere. Execution is everything, as Robespierre once observed, so we have to be persistent not just with the idea but in seeing it through to the bitter end. And I do mean bitter.

"Let me see if I can put it in a way that all of you can understand," mom said one day, lowering the guillotine on my father's proposal to open a cheesecake shop, never mind that none of us had any experience or knowledge of commercial baking. "Who's going to do the work?"

"Oh, well, I have school," said one.

"I have work," said another.

"I don't know how to bake," said a third.

"I'm allergic to cheese," said a fourth.

"Well, I'm not going to do the baking, so you can forget that right now. And I am not going to drive around delivering cheesecake at five in the morning!" mom declared.

She had a point. The idea seemed a little half baked, but that was how dad operated. He was more of an idea guy than a shop foreman, an inventor whose vision could not be contained by the laboratory walls around him. It's too bad he wasn't working during the heyday of Silicon Valley with its high-tech companies where you could ride around on scooters in the hallway and spend Friday afternoons tinkering on new projects like space elevators. Actually, I'm not sure that would have worked, either, because he never had much luck. He was persistent, but if you are in the wrong place at the wrong time with the wrong people for the wrong reason, all the persistence in the world won't make much difference. You have to have a feel for what will make a buck. Ah, right, that profit thing again.

"Face it, Art, if you ever went into the baby bonnet business, babies would be born without heads," mom said.

"What about all the houses I've bought and sold?"

"What about them? We've *lost* money on them!"

"The market dipped."

"I know what dipped. You're supposed to buy low and sell high, not the other way around."

"That's a riot. Maybe you should try standup."

Throughout my youth, there were ongoing jokes about "Buy High-Sell Low Real Estate," the unsuccessful beverage company known as "Six-Up," and "Arthur's Arthur Avenue Cheese Cake Shoppe," which was too long to fit on a standard business card. There were also lengthy arguments over how to spell "shop."

"So, tell me, do they even have cheesecake in England?" mom asked from out of nowhere, which was one of her endearments.

"What the hell has that got to do with anything?" dad said.

"Who else spells shop with two p's and an e?"

This was followed by extensive arguing and recollections of Uncle Angelo, who hated the British because of the Eighth Army pillaging everything in sight as it made its way up the eastern half of the Italian peninsula during World War Two. This included our family's village, Provvidenti. I bring this up as background to my own entrepreneurial efforts, the acorn not falling far from the tree, as they say. My inventive nature began to show itself in high school with the Mother's Day gift I made of a legless patio table (I hung it from a tree in the yard, but it had problems with balance, which seems to be an ongoing theme in my life). Like my father, I, too, have had bright ideas—*insights*, I prefer to call them—that have not panned out. Two major ones were the result of misery, the misery in both cases having one and the same source—cue Tammy Wynette's *D-I-V-O-R-C-E*. Not satisfied with one, I had to have two divorces, or, as mom put it, "two for the price of five. You're just like your father."

"Hey, I'm trying to find a girl just like the girl that married dear old dad."

"Good luck with that," my father said, shaking his head.

Divorce is a funny thing, "funny" as in the description of Jack Ripper in Stanley Kubrick's *Dr. Strangelove* (1964). The Air Force general had sent a squadron of B-52 bombers past their fail-safe points to start World War III, because he was, "you know, *funny*." Even though divorce may be described in the same way, it is funny for a different reason, mainly because it may be the only thing in life that is a true paradox. As such, it is accepted but not desired, understood but not fathomed, endured but not survived, forgivable but unforgiving, human but inhumane, finite but never ending, dying without death, and a transformed way of life that may not be much better than the former way. It is a different way that, in a lot of cases, turns out to be no different at all. Players get substituted in but the game remains the same. Woody Allen famously said that marriage is till death but an ex-wife is forever. Without waxing pathetic, let me just say that the misery of going through two divorces provided the motivation, inspiration, perspiration, migration, and every other "–ation" for launching my two bright ideas into business orbit. Well, my intentions were good. Cue The Animals, "I'm just a soul whose intentions are good. Oh, Lord, please don't let me be misunderstood."

Idea, the first: Pet Mat. Let me say, in case the reader is unaware, that there are various states of homelessness, from the truly destitute in rags pushing shopping carts down the street to the working poor who go to an office during the day but sleep at homeless shelters at night. In between, you can find people with no jobs or money but places to stay, those who work part-time and live in motel rooms with their kids, mentally unbalanced individuals without recourse to family or medical assistance, and drifters who don't fit in anywhere and are contemptuous of doing anything that might be construed as employment. The latter are often self-proclaimed Marxists who end up, at one point in their lives, in Santa Cruz, California, wearing tie dye and Bob Marley t-shirts. Because of Divorce Number One with Heidi, I fit somewhere in the middle: a forty-two--year-old doctoral student and father of three high-school aged girls writing his dissertation and teaching extra courses at the university on a contractual basis with no savings or home. For a while, I bounced from couch to couch with family, but once that got old and they changed the locks, I took to doing the only thing left to me: sleeping in my office. Talk about bringing your work home with you, or maybe your home work with you. I suppose in that way it was very convenient.

My office consisted of a dull, green room without windows on the third floor of an Aztec-looking building that was broad, flat, and ugly. It was the kind of room that got darker when you turned the light on, but it was roomy enough for me to stretch out in a sleeping bag and contemplate the smoldering wreckage of my life each night in the darkness. After a couple of times when the janitor hit my head opening the door at 1:00 am to collect the trash, I turned around so that my head was at the bookcase and my feet at the door. I had to get over my fear of books falling down on me in an earthquake, especially the massive tomes published by Oxford University Press like *The Complete History of History (Abridged Edition)*, but I figured an earthquake was the least of my worries. In fact, it would have been something to look forward to. My greatest fear was not being crushed to death but being found out by my colleagues. The shame would have been unbearable, even though the wage I was earning was ridiculously low, since I was not on tenure-track at the time. To make matters worse, I had been a student in the same program I was now teaching in, so people knew me and my work. I didn't want to ruin that by appearing as anything other than professional. Somehow, I had deemed homelessness unprofessional, sort of like bad form, probably after reading about the guy with a Ph.D. they found sleeping in his car in the parking lot at Stanford. That wasn't how I wanted to make a name for myself.

I knew I had to be clever, so I devised a system that allowed me to "leave" the office every night by 10:00 pm. At 9:45 I would go to the men's room, brush my teeth, floss, and force myself to pee, being careful not to let anyone see me with my shaving kit. Then I would go back to my office, pack my things, and leave. I would take the stairs down three flights to the first floor, cross the building to the west wing, go up that staircase to the third floor, walk down the hallway back to the east wing, and re-renter my office as quietly and inconspicuously as possible. I referred to it as my Nocturnal Rectangle, then my Rectal Nocturn. This was relatively easy to do, since night classes had ended by then and the janitorial staff hadn't started the graveyard shift yet. Once inside, I was careful not to make loud noises or turn the computer on for fear of being overheard. From that moment on, I was the Invisible Man, Ph.D. That meant that I couldn't leave until morning. So I used a series of paper coffee cups for drinking, rinsing, washing my face, and urinating, just in case someone ran into me on the way to the restroom in the morning. After all, I couldn't look like I had just spent the night in my office. I had to look refreshed and eager to discuss the latest departmental gossip. In academia, appearance is everything.[9]

This went on for the better part of a year. At one point, I got the flu for a week and taught classes drugged with an over-the-counter medication that I bought at the local grocery (I love codeine). I cancelled my office hours and sprawled out on the floor in my sleeping bag, shivering and sweating. As miserable as I felt physically, I missed my girls more. I did not split them up or make them leave the house, which they stayed in with their mother. I wanted life to continue as normal as possible, so I drove over the Santa Cruz Mountains several times a week to be with them and make whatever repairs I could on the house. "Divorce Italian style," my mother would say, shaking her head. What she didn't know was that there was a situation brewing with a neighbor several houses down. After repeated instances of verbal abuse, vandalism to our property, near fistfights, toe-to-toe yelling, threats on his part (veiled and not so veiled), and my searching him out in his favorite watering holes, I remembered Rocky and changed strategy. Since other neighbors on the street had been traumatized by him, I organized a group meeting with the local sheriff. When he started giving the deputies the same treatment, it was just a matter of time before they hauled him away in handcuffs. It made me realize that I needed to be close to the girls, who were thirty-five miles

---

[9] Later, as an Assistant Professor, I was fastidious in my appearance, often wearing a jacket and tie to class. Once, before class, I decided that my pants needed pressing, so I ironed them on the portable ironing board I kept by my desk. Unfortunately, I had left the door unlocked. A senior colleague knocked abruptly, opened the door, and found me standing there in a starched shirt, tie, jacket, shoes, socks, and silk boxers. After a pause she said, "It's so nice to see our new faculty taking such pains to look professional." Then she gently closed the door and left. We never spoke of it again.

away. When you've got three girls, even independent ones like mine, you do everything you can to protect them.

Enter the Hungarians. So that the reader may benefit as much as possible from the following description of Pet Mat, which I will get to eventually, let me explain that Hungarians are crazy. I will say it again so that there is no misunderstanding. Hungarians are crazy. I don't mean to suggest that some are crazy all of the time or even that all are crazy some of the time. I mean they are all crazy all of the time. I know it sounds harsh, but I am not trying to be mean or bigoted. I am just stating facts. They are contrary in nearly everything they do, from garbage collection to their views on the Federal Reserve Bank to their language. I suspect it has something to do with being related to the Mongols and one very famous Hun in particular, which is where they get their name. I used to think it was just my friend, the Hungarian Scout. He had very definite opinions about central banking and refused to pay for garbage collection, instead making weekly trips to the municipal garbage dump ten miles away. But then I realized the craziness wasn't limited to one individual. They are all crazy one way or another and so emotional that Italians, in comparison, look like Vulcans. They also have a lot of garlic in their diet, drink *pálinka*, which is their fruit-flavored brandy (my favorite is pear), and smother everything in sour cream. If that doesn't make you crazy, I don't know what will. Did I mention that I am an honorary Hungarian? It's true. Call me Magyar and put me on the list with Béla Lugosi, Béla Bartók, and Zsa Zsa Gabor.

Lest you think I have stepped beyond the pale, let me inform the reader that my friend and his family, though pureblood Magyar, are some of the most open-hearted and compassionate people I have ever met. They are quick to share everything they have, whether food, money, laughter, or time. I have known them for years, and in all that time their house has been open to all, from runaway kids to out-of-town relatives, bizarre religious pilgrims, and me in my hour of need. Actually, it was a year of need, like the queen's *annus horribilis*. They took me in just as the façade of hard-working academic burning the midnight oil began to crack and busybodies in the department were growing suspicious. The beginning of the end was the morning I was caught on my way to the men's room with a paper cup filled with urine. I treated it as if it were apple juice and stood ready to make the ultimate sacrifice but was saved at the last minute by our trusted administrative assistant and loyal friend.

The final straw broke in early summer when I went to the gym to shower at 6:00 am. They had turned off the hot water for the summer to work on a construction project, practically rebuilding the old facility from the inside out. So, I had gotten into the habit of going to the locker room early, stripping, soaping myself up, and rinsing off as quickly as possible in cold water. It wasn't a bad regime: cold water showers kept me from dwelling on the fact that I was homeless and lonely. It worked well until one morning when I had failed to notice the sign that said, "NO WATER AT ALL FOR 48 HOURS." That detail thing again. I discovered it only after I had soaped up and went to rinse off. The shower room consisted of an open space with columns, each column containing four showerheads. When the first showerhead didn't work, I went to the next. When all four didn't work, hissing and spitting water at me, I went to the next column. By the fifth column (!), after frantically rushing around twisting squeaky faucets, I slipped. I hit my head on the tiled floor and bruised my elbow. I managed to pick myself up and hobble over to the sinks, but no luck. I knew I had to act fast, because the track team would be arriving soon. That's when I realized that the only place with water was the toilet bowl. I picked the freshest-looking toilet I could find and rinsed off just before the boys showed up.

So my Hungarian friends, the Schmeringas, took me in and looked after me like a stray cat. A wet, stray cat. A wet, stray cat with fleas and diarrhea. For a year, I slept on the couch, floor, outside deck, spare bedroom, and army cot, which, finally, takes us to the invention of Pet Mat. I have written about this elsewhere but can tell you that Pet Mat is the result of two causes: (1) my (hyper) sensitivity to disgusting oral sounds, and (2) the Schmeringas' dog.[10] Regarding (1), I have nothing to say in my defense except that slurping, swallowing, sucking, gulping, gurgling, chewing, munching, crunching, sloshing, smacking, licking, biting, belching, and "croak throat" drive me crazy. That last one most often affects young women whose voices, for some reason, sound like the creaking deck of the Pequod. Maybe they think it's sexy, I don't know. These sounds are like kryptonite to me (not that I'm Superman or anything). I am not fond of hiccupping, either, although I wouldn't label it disgusting unless it is accompanied by sputtering discharges of air. For (2), suffice it to say that the Schmeringas loved dogs and could never be without at least one, occasionally two. Of the two Chihuahuas they currently have, one is evil and the other mentally deficient. But the one in particular that I am concerned with was the white poodle-spaniel-something or other mix that slept directly under my head as I lay in the cot and spent about an hour or so each night licking its testicles. Yes, it was male.

As if that weren't enough (it wasn't), the poodle-spaniel-something or other would go into the kitchen where it would slurp water from its bowl like a diabetic camel. It would drink a volume of water about twice its size over a period of

---

[10] In a shameless pitch of self-promotion, see Richard Mercurius' miraculous and near deadly inspiration for Pet Mat in *The Gringo* (New York: Blumen Publishing, 2011), 83.

approximately twelve minutes. Now, twelve minutes may not seem like a long time, but during the late night or early morning when everyone is asleep and nothing is stirring, not even a mouse, slurping tends to get magnified. Already on edge from the licking, I reacted to the slurping as if a burly Russian border guard were grinding rock salt into an open wound with the heel of his boot (only a slight exaggeration). But there was a ritual to the slurping that was even more insidious than the slurping itself. The dog would slurp the water, the feeding bowl would slide across the linoleum floor, and the dog would take a step closer for the next slurp, its nails clicking on the linoleum. So the ritual had a rhythm that went like this: slurp-slide-click, slurp-slide-click, slurp-slide-click. A person of sound mind would have ignored it, a reasonable man would have been asleep, someone with a home would have been in a proper bed and not the cot of a friend, but none of these conditions existed. I couldn't take it anymore. I jumped up (sprang from my bed to see what was the matter) and dashed into the kitchen. The dog stopped drinking to look up at me, its eyes innocent and welcoming. I don't know if it sensed what I had in mind, but I wanted to strangle it with my bare hands. The only thing that prevented me was the realization that it would have resulted in gurgling, choking, gasping, whining, and whimpering noises even worse than the original slurping. Then I composed myself. After all, I was an adult human being with an education. I had options. What were they, exactly? Again, I remembered Rocky. Think strategically, Brancatelli. That's when it hit me: Pet Mat!

Like a slap in the back of the head on a subway platform, I suddenly saw my salvation not in strangling the dog, crying myself to sleep, or even reconciling with Heidi, which would have been the mature thing to do, but in solving the problem of the slide. I couldn't stop the slurp, since the dog needed water, and I wasn't about to trim his nails, even if I could. The answer was obvious, at least standing in my underwear in the middle of the kitchen in the middle of the night: I had to stop the slide. I suppose this was another metaphor for my life, but I was in no mood for philosophizing. Besides, that's what had gotten me into the mess to begin with. And how would you stop the slide? Why, with a rubber mat fit securely beneath the feeding bowl composed of strategically designed suction cups to stick to any surface, including linoleum, that's how. Who needed a siege machine and flaming rockets when you had such a mat? And what would it be called if not "Pet Mat"? Not only would the torturous ritual end, but I would become rich marketing the invention to a world of pet-crazed Americans. The beast would get more water, I would get more sleep, and the country would get more enjoyment out of providing for their beloved animals. It was a win-win-win situation, not to mention the millions I would earn. I imagined myself being hailed as the "Pet Mat King." What could possibly go wrong?

My friend and I went to work immediately designing the suction cups, investigating possible manufacturers, and checking out the competition at places like Pet Smart, which had an entire aisle devoted to feeding bowls, dishes, cups, containers, receptacles, reservoirs, and time-released dispensers to prevent your pet from pigging out, unless, of course, your pet was actually a pig. There were even bowls with rubber bases that looked secure and may have prevented the bowl from sliding, but there was nothing as stable and innovative as vacuum-sealed suction cups. My friend, a mechanical engineer and inventor in his own right, having designed a water valve, faucet, pruning hook, laser site for a rifle scope, and a tape dispenser for picking cabbage, developed a prototype in his garage, which we took to a patent attorney. That's when we ran into trouble. When you dig deep enough into modern business, being careful to avoid the gas pipelines, you come across this bedrock principle: it takes money to make money. Don't let any post on Twitter or late-night infomercial shame you into thinking otherwise. You've got to have money and act as if you really don't care about it to make it. It's like playing hard to get, except for financial rather than romantic gain. You've got to make the banker, loan officer, investor, venture capitalist, customer, third cousin removed on your mother's side think that you couldn't care less if they funded your idea or not. In fact, you wish they wouldn't so you could take an early lunch. But you can't be cavalier about it, either. That's the trick. You have to show interest without showing interest. It's more like poker than anything else, which is why Pet Mat crashed and burned: not only am I unlucky in love, but at cards, too. I suppose if you're going to have nine lives, you end up paying for them one way or another.

Not able to afford the patent attorney, who was the kind of guy who sat in the basement of his office building eating liverwurst sandwiches with raw onions and surfing porn, we gave up. We flew the white flag of surrender, because we couldn't raise money for the patent search and product development. Needing money to make money is the only thing in the universe that works like that. Everything else requires other material to make. For water, you need atoms of hydrogen and oxygen. For table salt, sodium and chloride. Even my daughter, Rose, needs a molehill to make her mountain. You've got to have something to make something—only God can make something from nothing, *ex nihilo*, which is a good working definition of God as the Creator (Maker of Something from Nothing). Money is the only thing that makes itself, not having to rely on anything or anyone else, which could be the reason it causes so much trouble. Like Narcissus, it is in love with itself. In our case, it was so much in love with itself that it turned its back on me and my partner and slammed the door in our faces. Well, that's not entirely true. As a matter of fact, it's not true at all. We gave up on Pet Mat, because I moved into an apartment and didn't have to listen to slurp-slide-click anymore. Without the misery, I lost interest. Sayonara, Pet Mat. There, I feel much better even if supremely guilty.

Idea, the second: Snow Flow. This came out of Divorce Number Two, which was just as devastating as Divorce Number One, the effects of which continue to be felt today. In this regard (not to mention many others), Comrade Stalin of mass extermination fame was wrong. He said that when one man dies, it's a tragedy; when thousands die, it's a statistic. If you follow that logic, then Divorce Number Two should have been just a statistic, an unfortunate occurrence but nowhere near the tragedy of Divorce Number One. But it wasn't like that at all. I tell people who bother to ask (even I am bored talking about it) that it's more like two gunshot wounds. If you've been shot once, that won't prepare you for the second time around, even if it's with the same weapon under the same conditions. It's not as if the trauma suddenly gets reduced by half because you know the bullet caliber or point of entry. All of the anxiety, pain, bleeding, and tearing of flesh come back in spades. It's probably worse, because, really, who expects to get shot twice? I certainly didn't. It's like being hit by lightning twice. Sure, it happens, but only to people living on or near a golf course. So, my advice regarding divorce is not to live near a golf course. You also won't get into any sand traps that way.

Without getting into the hideous, horrific, and humiliating details, the second marriage ended with my wife, Katherine, leaving me and returning to California to be with her mother. We lived in Virginia at the time, having moved there after a series of tragic events that included, among other things, the loss of my job, Katherine's boss shooting himself after being arrested for insider trading, and my department chair's accidental death from electrocution. Not exactly a happy period in our lives. The two-year period 2008-2009 could be the worst time of my life. I say could, because I am still alive and who knows what's around the corner? I am not a pessimist; I just expect the worst. I also never expected to be back in Washington, DC. My marriage to Heidi ended after moving to DC on the Maryland side. My marriage to Katherine ended after moving to DC on the Virginia side. Our nation's capital has not been kind to me and my marriages despite all the rhetoric about family values and civic virtue. It's not that I blame DC for the divorces, you understand. It's just that something must happen to me whenever I get near cherry blossoms. If I ever move to Japan, I'll be in big trouble.

Katherine left after a great deal of huffing and puffing. She would take meandering walks around our suburban Alexandria neighborhood with the sheepdog we had adopted. Then she would argue with me about everything from the traffic on Telegraph Road to the mold in the basement, which was my fault. To be fair, I wasn't exactly on the short list for Husband of the Year. One day, I went for a walk and came upon her and the dog on the other side of the street. I ignored them as if they were strangers. This was the same woman I had promised to love and honor till I was termite dung. After she left I cried a Julie London song, mainly because I loved her but also because she left me with rent payments on a four-bedroom house, mortgage payments for the house we still owned in California, and a pile of credit card debt. Soon, I started having anxiety attacks. Whenever they passed, I would remember that I had to eat and would drive to the local supermarket and wander the aisles, listening to Karen Carpenter music and trying to find things like peanut butter and watermelon. Hint for those recently divorced: they're stocked in different places. Also, don't make the watermelon the first thing you pick up. Start with the peanut butter. Creamy or chunky doesn't matter.

To cut down on expenses, I moved into a house shared with three other guys, two of whom were in their mid-twenties, single, and smoked weed. Living with guys was stress-free and a welcome relief from the three months I had spent alone in the rented house, which I nicknamed the House of Doom. There was plenty of room in the basement, so I set up a man cave and attached all my refrigerator magnets to the furnace. I like to collect magnets from the places I've been, picking them up just before departure at the airport. I've got magnets from places like Pittsburg, Rome, Montreal, Kentucky, Belize, El Salvador, Rio de Janeiro, Mikonos, Dallas, Istanbul, Atlanta (A Peach of a City), Barcelona, Las Vegas, Chile, Seattle, Palm Springs, Minot in North Dakota,[11] and this little falafel place in Istinye, Turkey that motorcycle cops frequent, not to mention all of the colleges and universities I've been to for conferences and meetings. It was a colorful, eclectic display that I was very proud of, so much so that I would sit for hours admiring it. This was also when it would take me two hours to figure out which pair of socks to wear in the morning. Depression tends to do that. Then I burned all of the love letters I had written to Katherine but never mailed and nailed the charred remains to the support beams overhead. That still left scores of letters, emails, cards, poems, notes, and text messages already written and delivered to her to no avail—the woman was unmoved, sort of like an Unmoved Mover, whereas I was the object, the thing moved. Shoved, really. I may write a short story entitled, "Shoved, Really."

---

[11] I thought of a motto for Minot, North Dakota, which they pronounce "My-not," not "Meeno" as *en français*. It could go on refrigerator magnets, bumper stickers, the letterhead of the local Chamber of Commerce, and the road sign welcoming visitors to their fair city. It was, "Why not Minot?" I probably should have gone into marketing. I think I'm a natural. If you're ever in My-not, get yourself over to the "Roll 'n Pin" restaurant. Why not?

I spent a year in this bachelor pad with the guys. The twenty somethings were gone a lot, which left me to mope in misery with the third guy, a friend of mine whom I had met working at yet another dysfunctional job on "K" Street near Georgetown. We would commiserate about loves lost, the workings of the female mind, family, the control freaks at work, and divorce. This led to our conclusion that what the country needed was a resurgence of true masculinity. We wanted to save it from those spineless guys who wore "Yes, Dear" t-shirts. The first step in our campaign was to write a book entitled *Jesus' Penis*, which would be an analysis and critique of why Jesus is always depicted in a loincloth on the cross but never naked. We were convinced after Googling images from every artistic period and studying my highlighted sections of Burton Throckmorton's *Gospel Parallels* that a conspiracy was afoot not just to deny Jesus' masculinity but to undermine the "testicular nature" of the Incarnation. Granted, many people already have trouble with that aspect of the Incarnation, but we weren't talking about seminarians in cassocks. We wanted real, honest, musk-based salvation. It fell apart when I came home early one day and found him watching *Annie* with the curtains drawn. He had been crying. That's when I realized, of course, that Jesus was circumcised. I also realized that there was something odd about a fifty-year-old man living with roommates and writing penis books. This coincided with an opportunity to move to New York, so I took it, but not before spending one more winter in Virginia.

Now, it just so happens that the winter of 2010 included some monster blizzards called, collectively, "Snowmageddon" that dumped more than three feet of snow and shut down the Metro rail and bus system for days. It reminded me of the snowstorms we had in Wheaton, Maryland years earlier. How long can four guys survive in one house during the mother of all snowstorms? As it turns out, not nearly as long as that nineteenth-century, Arctic expedition in search of the Northwest Passage when the ship's crew got lead poisoning, went crazy, and then ate each other. We were close to eating each other after just three days. By then, I had had enough of board games, cards, puzzles, ESPN, hip hop music, arm wrestling, grab-assing, penis jokes, putdowns, arguing over dishes, bitching about women, boasting about women, farting, belching, beer guzzling, shots of tequila, doing laundry, and long phone calls home. When the boys decided to play a medley of Eminem hits on their homemade, bamboo flutes, I buttoned-up my overcoat and went outside to shovel.

I searched the basement, shed, and backyard, but the only tools I found were for gardening and barbequing. So I stood there, as I usually do, not knowing what to do. That's when I noticed some plastic patio furniture sticking out of the snow, the kind you don't mind leaving behind when you move. One of the chairs lay on its back, which was flat and wide like the blade of a snow shovel. Its four legs stuck out parallel to the ground with just enough space for me to stand in between. So, I did. Then I got this wild idea and took it to the front to see if I could shovel with it. To my surprise, the back of the chair plowed through the newly-fallen snow, churning it over on either side. It was like the prow of a ship coursing through water or a farmer's plow tilling soil. It turned out to be an almost perfectly designed, light-weight snow plow. I cleared the walkway, driveway, and sidewalk down to the corner, then back again. It was the easiest thing in the world, even with more snow falling.

After a while, I must have looked ridiculous, because I heard a voice calling out.

"Hey, what are you doing?"

On the other side of the street stood a guy in a parka, scarf, and aviator bomber cap. He looked like somebody from

I found an invention company that promised to help us design, manufacture, market, and distribute "SnoFlo." Naturally, they were very excited about all the money that was to be made and dazzled me with images of late-night, cable TV ads like the ones for steak knives and vegetable juicers. I was flattered but remembered my job interview in Monterey and how I had been sucker punched. I let them court me, anyway. To be honest, I enjoyed the attention. Backstage, though, things started falling apart when they demanded that the "F" in SnoFlo be lowercase, claiming that "it looked cleaner." I insisted on uppercase and held my ground. It was a matter of principle. After all, who was the inventor here? Who had suffered through that harsh winter of discontent and snatched fortune from the fangs of divorce? In addition, my partner and I were looking at thousands of dollars in fees for a patent attorney and membership dues just to join this exclusive group of losers. Not only that, but since the manufacturer would be taking on risk, I was told that he would want a substantial cut of the profit, too. Everybody seemed to have their hands in our pocket, and, when all was said and done, we were said and done. I got the feeling that if I had pitched them with an idea for bamboo musical instruments, the results would have been no different. The company was about as reliable as an Enron annual report but not nearly as clever.

Better to end the tale here, leaving you, the reader, with much to consider regarding misery and roads paved with good intentions, which is what started all of this in the first place. Whether my own misery was self-inflicted or created is something I will have to think about. If created, then I wonder from what, considering the aforementioned principle of nothing from nothing. It would mean that either the material for my misery was already there, the result of family conditioning and early childhood socialization, or floating around double-helix-like in the mitochondrial soup of Robbie's soul. That's a foul thought. Can a person carry his own destruction within him? Was I destined to run from showerhead to showerhead in sudsy despair? I do not know. The only thing I know is that it happened. I rinsed myself off in a toilet bowl, which is not exactly like Anita Ekberg splashing around in the Trevi Fountain, but it was iconic nevertheless, at least *pour moi*. I am just glad that it was early enough in the day for no one else to see. I have to focus on what to do with what I have, limited though it may be. It doesn't matter whether I inherited it, earned it, stole it, or found it inside a paper bag in the bus terminal.

The moral of this story, which many of us already know, is that when kicked in the teeth by misery, whether from divorce, bankruptcy, mutant viruses, enemies with crystal balls and flying monkeys, a 5x10 cell, invention swindlers, or anything else, you climb back up on your saddle and keep riding, cowboy. You get misery back by not giving up, by wandering around the supermarket like a demented Mafia don until you get a charley horse from carrying a twelve-pound watermelon with an image of Katherine's face on it. That's how you learn. That's how you grow. Success, dear reader, is irrelevant, an insignificant and ultimately meaningless byproduct of persistence, of suiting up every day and going out there to get kicked in the teeth. If you are put off by that, then don't think of it as masochism or self-sabotage. Think of it as your dental plan.

These Boots Are Made

for Walkin

Speaking of Anita Ekberg and fountains, there's another film from that same period of Italian cinema that is a work of genius and defines how I approach romance and love. If that doesn't make you drop everything and run to Netflix, I don't know what will. No, it's not sci-fi. The film is *La Ragazza con la Valigia* (The Girl with a Suitcase) and was made in 1961, which is portentous in itself, since 1961 is one of those rare numbers that looks the same upside down as right-side up. I am not a numerologist, but what could be more telling than that?[12] I look for that kind of symmetry constantly, yet I am not a superstitious guy and know that, while there is a great deal of significance in numbers, numbers are a bunch of fa-la-la-la-la, because we made them up. By "we," I mean human beings. I am not aware of any animals using numbers, although squirrels may, in fact, have devised some sort of numeric system to keep track of their nuts (or the total tonnage of birdseed consumed).

---

[12] I must give credit where it is due. This idea is not mine but taken from Richard Mercurius in one of his internal monologues. See *The Gringo*, p. 185. If you are truly interested in numerology, see Underwood Dudley, *Numerology: Or What Pythagoras Wrought* (Washington, DC: Mathematical Association of America, 1997). No, I am not making this up.

We made up 1961, along with 1960 and 1962, which is also the year of a certain fin-tailed Ford Thunderbird I used to own just like my Hungarian friend, who is also named Robert. His son is Robert, too, although not a junior, if such a thing is possible. What are the odds of that? Whenever I called the house and the son answered, I would say, "Robert? This is Robert. Is Robert there?" Did that for years, never got old (not to me, anyway). Do you see how significant all of this is? Sure you do, until you realize that it isn't, because I have come to learn that patterns are like trapping the wind, as they say in *Ecclesiastes*, or pinpointing the position of a subatomic particle to put it in modern terms. According to the Heisenberg Uncertainty Principle—which I live by, by the way—as soon you locate the position of a subatomic particle, the act of locating it moves the particle so that you can never really be sure where it is. How frustrating is that? It's like trying to strain a gnat from a glass of iced tea, or a Greek myth, which is more than appropriate considering the names for these little bits of mass-matter-momentum-energy come from Ancient Greek. To me, it's just another version of angels dancing on the head of a pin. Maybe that's not what the guys at the Fermilab want to hear, but it is what it is, as they say in my neighborhood, which has plenty of guys named Angel.

But to get back to the girl with the suitcase, Valerio Zurlini's incredible film about young love, there is a scene in which sixteen-year-old Lorenzo watches a twenty-something Aida glide down the staircase in a bathrobe with her hair wrapped in a towel. The famous tenor, Beniamino Gigli, sings the aria "Celeste Aida" as she floats down the staircase. Lorenzo is played by a wispy Jacques Perrin and Aida by Claudia Cardinale, who weighed more than him even back then. Lorenzo is transfixed by her beauty, her mystery, and Verdi's music. Aida, reacting to Lorenzo and feeling naked, draws the bathrobe tighter around herself. Their emotions are so raw that they have to look away momentarily; hers is a blush of self-consciousness, his a pensive distraction. You can almost imagine him later that night trying to figure things out on a slide rule. *Quid fit?* What is going on? They are both, as Virgil says of Dido, *caeco carpitur igni,* wasted with fire unseen (*The Aeneid* 4.2). The inevitability of their love becomes obvious as the story unfolds, finally reaching its climax in a beach scene. This, despite their differences in social class, upbringing, and age. Lorenzo is driven by his obsession for and fascination with Aida. Aida realizes that the only man in her life who truly loves her is a boy. The tender moment they share is intense but fleeting. Their love is meant to be but only for a moment. Their parting scene at a train station (where else?) is punctuated by the shrill whistle of the train and the rhythmic clanging of its bell.

Verweile doch! Du bist so schön!

Now, here's the thing: I am not sixteen. I am closer to sixty-one than sixteen; same numbers, different order. How did it happen? I have no idea. For the longest time, I was the youngest guy in the room and then all of a sudden I was the oldest. It was like being in a meeting, getting up to use the men's room, and coming back thirty years later. I don't even do drugs. Now, this may be nothing more than an issue of hair dye or Botox for some people. Others may have a midlife crisis and ride a red motorcycle through Patagonia, but I am at my psychic limit on that account, having had my midlife crisis from twenty-three to fifty-one, as already noted, when I really did have a motorcycle (a black Nighthawk). So I have to come up with another reason to explain why I am as enthralled by the movie as much as Lorenzo was by Aida on the staircase. If my understanding of attraction and love is closer to sixteen while my physical age is closer to its inverse, then I am in big trouble. In this regard, numbers mean everything. You might say they count, but I am above the cheap laugh. The truth is that I am attracted to the grand finale, the Kirk Gibson homerun, the overtime touchdown, the boom-puff-sizzle of July Fourth, the *coup de foudre* lightning bolt of love, Beatrice at the bridge, Juliet at the balcony, Helen at the parapet, and Sinatra's crowded room with strangers exchanging glances as the band played on. In short, I am an idiot. But it's not the end of the world, because being an idiot is one thing, thinking you're something else quite another. I know I am an idiot, which is half the battle—the rear half—but half nevertheless.

Please, do not misunderstand me. This isn't about my being a hopeless romantic, nor even a hopeful one, since I've never denied that life is anything but harsh. But it is precisely because of its harshness that I look for a little magic every now and then. And by magic, I don't mean shopping at Macy's. That's not so bad, is it? Isn't that the human condition: striving to create magic out of the harshness of the elements, poverty, hunger, inhumanity, violence, and most social institutions whose sole aim is to drive you out of your skull?

"Life is about losing," Lena explained to Daniella years after the piano bench incident when Daniella ran and lost for class president.

"See, we're all losers, but losing is part of life. It's how you prepare to win. Without losing, you'll never learn how to be a winner. So, even though you lost the election, what do you say we go out for a cheese burrito?"

Needless to say, my daughter is not good at pep talks. Volunteering at a suicide prevention hotline would not be a good idea. I felt it my duty to step in with the historical perspective, what with my being the family historian and all. So, I reminded Daniella of the failures and losses suffered by Abraham Lincoln—a sweetheart dying, a nervous breakdown, losing election after election, and the toll the Civil War took on him, ultimately costing him his life ("the occasion is piled high with difficulty"). I believe this helped soften the blow. Still, I could tell it was painful for her, although nowhere near as painful as it was for Lena. And I know that, like a gunshot wound, the next loss won't be any easier. There is always hope even when reality stares us in the face and jumps up and down, trying to get our attention. Hope is the last thing to die, *l'ultima a morire*, if it dies at all, surviving even longer than cockroaches after an atomic explosion. Why? Because we are built for greatness, to share in something greater than ourselves, something that makes us immortal. Doesn't Achilles choose death on the battlefield and thus obtain for himself immortal fame over a long but boring existence as a farmer staring at the butt end of an ox? I believe that we are wired for the long ball, for swinging for the fences, for sitting on that one pitch that's going to change everything. How can it be otherwise?

Speaking of atomic explosions, which are initiated through a triggering device, I must admit that I, too, have a triggering device. My heart pounds in a romantic rush and the detonation sequence begins whenever I am in the presence of boots. That's boots, not boobs. I don't mean boots at the department store, although they, too, can be a huge turn-on (especially their smell) but boots in more specific terms as when there is someone filling them. I have always been fascinated by them, all of them: leather, suede, patent, motorcycle, harness, Wellington, thigh-high, knee-high, calf-high, zippered, laced, cowboy. That reminds me of the time I bought my first pair of cowboy boots at Tony Lama's in San Antonio and wore them all day at the Alamo, then up and down the River Walk. When I got back to the hotel, my feet were in shreds. I considered calling 911 to have the boots removed surgically.

"Don't you know you have to break them in?" a local guy said, incredulous.

Actually, the salesman warned me about breaking them in, but I thought that only applied to baseball mitts and motorcycles. Okay, so I was wrong (see "Bloomington" for my being wrong about everything). Despite that painful experience

(I would rather have been attacked by Santa Ana's men), I remain drawn to boots and can remember a time when women wore go-go boots and Catwoman was played by actresses like Eartha Kitt and Julie Newmar. They not only wore boots but purred, meowed, and slunk about Gotham City in leather jumpsuits as I held my pubescent breath inches from the television set, fogging up the tube. I have an active imagination. My first party outside the school gym was in 1970 in the basement of Judy Pericone's house. Judy wore white lipstick with white boots to match. I still remember dancing with her to Herb Alpert's *This Guy's in Love with You*. And I was, I swear, for the four and-a-half minutes of the song. Maybe even a week afterward.

So, for me the triggering device to love and romance has been boots. They are what jumpstart my journey into Ga-Ga-Land. But they are also what lead me down the path of destruction like sirens on the rocks. That's mixing metaphors again, but think of me as Aeneas traveling the Mediterranean in search of a new homeland constantly harassed by the goddess Juno, who is pissed off at the Trojans and wants all of them dead at the bottom of the sea. Okay, so maybe I'm not Aeneas, but the boots might just as well have been sent by a pissed-off goddess. Consider the pair and the woman in them that lured me into a brief encounter of whirlwind proportions only to end when both boots and woman kicked me (literally) out of her apartment into the drafty hallway. The scary thing is that the wearer's prior involvement in human trafficking hadn't put me off. I went ahead anyway. What's a little plea bargaining with a federal prosecutor compared to white, leather hip boots with laces tied up the back? I might as well have been at the bottom of the sea. Or the time I fell for a pair of suede, fringed boots worn by a frisky redhead with an unstable personality who demanded that I prove my undying love for her by dying. When I pointed out the illogic of that she went Juno ballistic and hurled thunderbolts at me. Or the dancer from Senegal who left her blue, suede boots at my apartment who charged me with being inattentive and unloving. I can't offer much of a defense. I don't like having to check in every evening as if I were on a stakeout. I don't even like talking on the phone (something I inherited from my father). Maybe I've been living alone too long.

The odd thing (no, we haven't gotten to it yet) is that neither one of my wives wore boots. They weren't the boots type. Is there such a thing? Maybe, or maybe there is a boots mood or a boots event that allows for, even demands, boots. I'm not talking about equestrian shows unless you consider Belmont an equestrian show. I am saying that neither Heidi nor Katherine were that type, which is significant, because it may mean that, although I go ga-ga over blue suede boots, I know they don't last and that the people filling them are not "marriage material." I don't like putting it that way, but women say that all the time, so in the interest of fairness, I will let it stand. If this is true, it leads to a bigger question: "What on earth is the triggering device for?" Is it to warn me about the women I should *not* marry (booted females—give them the boot!), or does it simply call attention to the stupidity of my hormones? Wait, may it please the court: the stupidity of my choices based on my hormones. There, that's better. Or, even more interesting, is it a vestige from an early evolutionary period when there was a need to find healthy, reproducible females (the booted ones) and mate with them to ensure offspring? Now, however, it serves as nothing more than a kind of sexual appendix or tonsil with no discernible purpose other than to cause chaos. That would be nice, especially since it would absolve me of moral responsibility, for how could I be held accountable for a little wiggly thing in my side or two red blotches at the back of my throat, metaphorically speaking, that is.

All right, now comes the odd thing, and I have Lena to thank for it: Lena, the child who has witnessed everything and attended all of my weddings (we'll leave out the details). Not only did she make the Einstein volleyball team at five feet, two inches, but she had sufficient presence of mind to conclude at the end of her father's second marriage that he has a penchant for what she called "crazy eye." It's probably worth putting in initial capital letters: Crazy Eye. And she was right. What I had mistakenly judged to be love was, in a word, craziness. See, the problem with boom-puff-sizzle is that once the fireworks end, everybody packs up their lawn chairs and goes home. You can't stand there waiting for more or expect similar fireworks the next morning at the office. But my problem was more than expectations gone awry. It was a major malfunction in that part of the brain responsible for mature and informed judgment. I can remember falling and hitting my forehead as a teenager and then, later, getting stung by that swamp fly, also in the forehead. I think that's what happened. My judgment became impaired as a result of frontal lobe trauma. I am probably eligible for government assistance and a motorized wheelchair with an orange pennant.

On the other hand, maybe it's time to man-up, as they say (*Jesus' Penis*). I can't blame evolution, frontal lobe trauma, or boots. Well, boots I can blame. They would drive any man crazy. Even so, it's time to stand up and pay the piper, fiddler, pizza guy, etc. Crazy Eye is the result of viewing emotional instability and pathology on the part of certain women as love. Of course, I am also open to the possibility that the instability and pathology may be my own, but that's the subject of another book. One woman, an exotic, self-proclaimed witch, showed up for our first date with a broom and a box of cannoli. The cannoli were great, not too creamy and containing just the right amount of ricotta.

My mother has asked, "Where do you meet these women—the parking lot of outpatient clinics?"

As you may have guessed, sensitivity does not run in my family, not unless we've been slighted in some way. We met at a church car wash, the witch and I. I removed my glasses, flashed my green eyes at her, and made some witty remark about fenders. You can imagine the rest. We lasted several months and then revived it one year later. It was revived by me, which lends credibility to the frontal lobe theory, because only a mentally impaired man would walk through a burning building twice. Then she dumped me, accusing me of being self-righteous, misogynistic, and completely detached from my emotions.

"Your point?" I asked.

She gasped, sputtered, wheeled about, and slammed the door. I still have the broom.

What's interesting is that I only want what everybody else wants: companionship. To come home to someone I love and eat chili with raisins and sauvignon blanc and then hold that person in bed through the night is a dream come true. All right, so we can change the menu, but, really, all I want is companionship. Companionship and sex. Companionship and sex, because, after all, where do you think all that cuddling is leading? And a nice house. You can't do all of that in a shack in Albany, California or Albany, New York, or a Waffle House anywhere. You have to have the right ambience, which means a living room, dining room, three bedrooms, two toilets, detached garage, and a yard with a hot tub that is obstructed as much as possible from the views of prying neighbors. It also has to have hardwood floors (have you ever heard of softwood?), stained glass windows, and a bannister. My grandmother's house on Staten Island had a terrific bannister that we used to ride down like little firemen. And the house has to be in Napa. I love grapes and wine and, as I mentioned, chili. That's not too much to ask for: companionship, sex, a house in Napa, and someone easy to be with. I forgot about that. You can't be with someone who is so much work that your hair starts to fall out. I'm not talking about arguing, because, after all, arguing is foreplay. Wait, that's what I thought with Katherine. Funny thing, but in her mind, arguing meant arguing, not foreplay. The more it turned me on, the more distraught she became. I thought those were tears of joy. Then the knives came out.

It's obvious that I have a way with women. I don't like to brag, but it's true. It may not be the right way, but it is still a way.[13] There are three reasons for this: (1) Tammy Wynette. Need I say another word about divorce, which is an experience not unlike a beginner skier taking the black diamond run down the mountain? I think not. Since I don't ski, I can only remember turning a toilet bowl into the Trevi Fountain and how stupendous that felt; (2) New York, the Big Apple, Gotham, the City that Never Sleeps, Knickerbocker Town, If You Can Make it There You Can Make it Anywhere. When you live there, you learn pretty quick (in a New York minute) how to get to the heart of things; and (3) rearing daughters. People have their opinions about boys versus girls and which are easier to bring up. Since I didn't have boys, I can't compare, although looking back at what my mother went through makes me think girls are easier. Some people with girls will gasp in horror at that, but I'm starting to think that there are hard and easy parents, not children. I hear the sound of helicopter blades almost everywhere I go nowadays.

---

[13] Recall George Sanders' line to Marilyn Monroe in *All About Eve* (1950). Marilyn had just called the butler a waiter and defended herself by saying, "Well, I can't yell "Oh butler!" can I? Maybe somebody's name is Butler." Sanders conceded, "You have a point. An idiotic one, but a point."

Okay, so divorce (1) had the extremely painful effect of breaking me in like a pair of Tony Lama boots on the River Walk. Up to that point, I was my own man; not quite an ass but not a saint, either, even after three kids, which should have been enough to tame the wild hair in any man. But I am not any man. I am emotionally and psychologically stunted in that I react to things at a much slower pace than other people and am, by most accounts, a late bloomer. So, even marriage and fatherhood weren't enough to mold me into a mature, responsible adult. For that, I needed Divorce Number One, during which I showered at the gym and spent every morning trying to figure out where I would sleep in the evening. But peeing in coffee cups got old, as I have recounted. Eventually, I turned myself around hokey pokey-like and learned something about compassion in the process. For instance, I don't look at homeless people the same way anymore. I can remember years later when Katherine and I were walking down Peachtree Street in Atlanta and took a homeless man to dinner. I don't think I would have done that before experiencing Divorce Number One and the generosity of the Hungarians. I also learned that there are about a hundred and eleven thoroughfares of one kind or another named "Peachtree" in Atlanta. Without Divorce Number One, I wouldn't have been in Atlanta at all and certainly not with Wife Number Two.

Divorce Number Two with Katherine was even more complicated, since it involved two levels of immaturity, mine and hers, not that I blame her since her immaturity derived from the fact that she was more than twenty years my junior. I have left that detail out, mainly because it could take up an entire book by itself. In case you might be thinking what I think you might be thinking, don't think it. Katherine was not the cause of Divorce Number One and arrived on the scene much later, playing Heloise to my Abelard. However, since those scars are recently healed-healing-will be healed, I have no intention of opening them up again for the edification or entertainment of those in the balcony. Suffice it to say that Divorce Number Two taught me to be a kinder, gentler man. Katherine had accused me of being cruel and unusual (she was a lawyer). I accepted the charge of being unusual (can a man deny that the sun comes up every morning?) but resolutely denied being cruel. Besides, her idea of cruelty was my telling her not to skip down the stairs when we had company over. That reminds me of dear old mom's comment about what to get her for Christmas the first year we were together.

"How about a pair of roller skates?"

Moving to New York City from Virginia (2) during the summer of 2010 toughened me up. I've learned to be guarded with my time. I am also guarded with my energy, money, and resources. Frankly, I can't waste time anymore with people who just want to complain, argue, act out, create drama, use me, pump me for information, borrow my car (not that I have one anymore), pontificate, draw me into their delusions, get me to work for free, get me to take them to dinner, drop their pants and defecate all over my shoes (a version of who can piss farther), or couldn't care less whether I am dead or alive. I have met very few women in New York who weren't either crazy or so self-absorbed that they could have been on a date with themselves. Often, they were both. I don't think it's just the women I meet or attract, either. There's something going on beyond my little corner of the Big Apple; maybe it's the water. When I say this to women, they tell me that there are a lot of crazy men out there, too. I believe them, which is why the New York experience has made me harder and wiser about how I spend my time, whom I spend it with, and where it's spent. There's a lot of spending going on in that sentence, but I figure it's an appropriate metaphor if you think of yourself as having so many gold coins in life. You don't want to waste them. The upshot of all this is that I don't date a lot. I'm probably not alone there. Well, I am, but you catch my drift. But it's better to be alone than tortured together.

"What are you doing with these women? It's time to shit or get off the pot," my father would say, evoking that New York ethos.

"Leave him alone, would you? You know he has irritable bowel," my mother would reply in my defense.

There's a photo on my credenza of my three daughters as toddlers (3). They are standing at the back door of our house in San Jose staring at the camera with a mixture of curiosity and trust as if to say, "We have no idea what you two are up to with that thing in your hands, but we will stand here and await instructions. Why are you laughing so hard?" The twins are more or less equal in height, chubby, dimpled, and sporting mixing bowl haircuts ("Hair by Dad"). Lena is a good four inches taller. I hope she enjoyed it. That was the last time she was the tallest. As an adult, Deanna is five feet, eleven inches compared to Lena's five feet, two inches. Rose is an Aristotelian mean at five feet, six inches, which is fitting since she is the middle child and a Philosophy major. The fact that one of my daughters is taller than me and another shorter than my grandmother is poetic. Genes are the great equalizer. I cherish the photo because it is iconic.

As parents, we have a fixed image in our minds of our children: their ages, faces, hair, bodies, clothes, how they move, how they speak. That one image comes to mind whenever we think of them, as if it were an icon for a mobile phone app. It doesn't matter if they are fifteen or fifty, that image is set in stone, an amber encased specimen from an earlier time that is preserved forever in our minds. Often, it is the image we react to rather than the person standing in front of us. That isn't always so bad, because as time slips by the past goes with it, and we are left with words instead of the reality the words represent. "Remember when" takes the place of what we are trying to remember. We are left with memories of memories like mirrors facing each other, the reality lost in infinite reflection. I think again of the onion and the night the redwood branch fell on our roof in Capitola. The redwood tree is gone; "our" roof is gone; even the elm trees in San Jose that towered over us as we took the photo at the back door are gone, the victims of Dutch elm disease. This would be a horrifying experience if not for daughters, who are tough on the outside but tender on the inside and will do anything for you if you show them that you love them. As Psalm 128 says, they are like olive plants around your table. Well, if olive plants could yell and argue over clothes.

Even so, I fear I am rough on women, booted or not. Washington, DC may have been the litmus test, with one wife surviving the pioneer experience and the other succumbing to the elements in the frozen wasteland of Alexandria, Virginia. DC was the test, but I was the one who brought them there, only afterward realizing just how hard it is for a West Coast native to live in the East. It was like taking a gazelle from the grasslands and putting it in a cage at the Bronx Zoo. Captivity destroys the spirit. It is much easier to go the other way, from the East to the West. I am a perfect example of this, even though for the first five years living in California I couldn't open my mouth without someone taking offense. The funny part is that most of the time I wasn't trying to offend anybody. Well, some of the time. Maybe it was one time. It's not that I didn't care or was heartless. I just couldn't believe that all of that sun-tanned skin could be so thin. I don't know why I didn't believe it; all I had to do was look at my own family. To tell you the truth, after a while I enjoyed it.

I probably won't ever tell her, but the witch was right about my being detached from my emotions. It comes from spending years in my grandmother's basement. You see, I would go there to escape the chaos swirling above me. My grandmother on my father's side (of Mother Matter fame) lived in the Rosebank section of Staten Island close to St. George where the famous, orange ferry docks and occasionally smashes into pilings. She had a limp from childhood polio and was my grandfather's second wife, which was practically unheard of at the time (1920s). The story goes that my grandfather's first wife was Spanish and feisty, perhaps a Gypsy, maybe a werewolf, and that the marriage did not last long. It's possible that the troop transport, instead of going to England, was diverted to Spain via Gibraltar because of the war ending. If so, he could have met her there and had trysts at Alcazaba. That is pure conjecture on my part; he could also have met her on his rounds in Spanish Harlem collecting garbage, which would have made her Puerto Rican. It's been rumored that the marriage produced a child, a girl, but I don't know anything about her. My grandmother once said that the reason she married a divorced man was that no one else would have her because of her limp.

I would seek refuge in my grandmother's basement from the following: my father yelling, my grandfather yelling, my grandmother yelling, my uncle yelling, my grandfather coughing up a lung and depositing it in the bottom half of a Borden's Milk carton that he kept at the side of the couch where he spent most of the time I knew him (he also wore ball caps long before it was fashionable), my grandmother arguing with him in Italian, my uncle pacing the floor and cursing in a loud voice at the little people escaping every orifice of his body and then at Huntley and Brinkley on the six o'clock news, the radio blaring, the coffin-sized phonograph turning out everything from Italian ballads by guys named "Nicky" and "Johnny" to Engelbert Humperdinck, the canaries my grandmother kept chirp-chirp-chirping and then screeching whenever my father hurled a throw-pillow at them ("What the hell else are they for?"), and the comings and goings of five mentally disabled teenagers from Willowbrook State School that my grandmother cared for. One of them, Freddie Gonzalez, nearly died falling through a storefront window and another, John Williams, did a tour of duty in the army in Vietnam, no troop transport delays for him. In addition, my uncle played the piano by ear and was very good at it. Once, though, off his meds, he came downstairs stark naked, sat down at the upright (the piano), and played *Pennies from Heaven* until my father made him go back to his room. It wasn't pretty. I still shudder whenever I hear that song. Or see a penny.

The basement had a few things going for it other than the fact that it wasn't upstairs. Now that I think of it, we had our own version of *Upstairs Downstairs* going on at the time. To wit, it was cool in the summer, dimly lit with sunshine coming through the windows from the street, and quiet. You entered through a pair of French doors that had nearly every pane broken, and—here's the kicker—it was filled with books. I mean stacks of them, everywhere, from floor to ceiling. There were also bookshelves covering the walls stuffed with books of all kinds. At first, it was hard to move around, like being in a cave of book stalagmites, but eventually I cleared a spot for myself in a corner. It was my first man cave. I suppose it is true that men spend their lives trying to sneak back to the womb, which explains Nicodemus' question to Jesus when told that he had to be born again to enter the Kingdom of God: "How can a person once grown old be born again? Surely he cannot reenter his mother's womb and be born again, *can he?*" (John 3:4). Notice that he says *can he*. You get the feeling he really wants to know, hoping that Jesus can tell him. Give me a man cave, he pleads. Adding insult to injury, Jesus says, "You are the teacher of Israel and you do not understand this?" (3:10).

We spent most Sundays at my grandmother's, so after a few weeks in the basement I decided to crack open a book that looked interesting. It was *Ivanhoe* and had a green cover and tissue paper covering each illustration. It took a while to get through the "thou and thine" of it, but once Wamba called himself an "ass," I was hooked. This was followed by *The Scarlet Pimpernel, Edwin Drood,* a collection of short stories by Robert Louis Stevenson, an illustrated series on lepidoptera (180,000 species), Carl Jung's *Book of Dreams* (glossy pages), an elementary German reader with drawings of a guy with a monocle who looked like Monopoly Man, and *The Encyclopedia Britannica*. I read them all or tried to read them all. I didn't quite go the distance with the encyclopedia, quitting once I got to "XYZ." What could be in that volume except for Zebra and Zeppelin? Actually, there was a picture of the Hindenburg exploding at Lakehurst, New Jersey, which was cool. I had to reread the section on the physics of television a couple of times, because, as my uncle was ranting at it one afternoon, clothed, I realized I had no idea how it worked and decided not to watch it again until I had at least a rudimentary understanding of wave theory. This took a while, because I had to work through the theories about the Hindenburg disaster first (I liked the oxyhydrogen one). I'm sure I missed out on some great episodes of *Star Trek* and *Get Smart*, but it was for the good of science. One has to make sacrifices. Meanwhile, the volumetric pressure on my young brain was enormous.

As the years passed, I advanced from one stalagmite of knowledge to another, and, thanks to all that reading, went to college as a callow youth of seventeen, bright-eyed and ready to explore the world of the intellect. Little did I know that I was trading one form of craziness for another, but that's best left for a second volume of nine lives. That would bring the total to eighteen, which is significant from a numerological standpoint, although what that significance is I do not know. All of the lives and stories ought to be about craziness, because that's what life is—a series of crazy events. Or is it?

One thing I have learned is that you don't have to be afraid of craziness, because in the end the only thing fear does is move you further away from love, which is not where you want to be on your deathbed (or any other bed). For instance, my cousin, not having had the benefit of a magical basement, learned this lesson the hard way. She took drugs to escape the craziness, once boasting that she had been in every jail from San Jose to Fresno (her family made that California trip during the 1960s, never to return). That was probably the quaaludes talking, but it is true that she belly-flopped into the crazy end of the pool while I dabbled my toes at the kiddie end. It's not that I found craziness without a certain charm. I even wanted to be part of it. I was just terrified of drowning. So, I studied it from afar, adopting a Mr. Spock (may he rest in peace) attitude toward everything in life that had a whiff of craziness to it. Well, everything except for that one Achilles heel of mine. But I suppose things could have turned out worse. Instead of Nancy Sinatra's *These Boots Are Made for Walkin,* it might have been *Bang Bang.* I'm just lucky that way.

Mamma Mia

(*not* ABBA or a Broadway musical)

"—forgive, I pray thee, this rash humour which my mother gave me."

Laurence Sterne, *The Life and Opinions of Tristram Shandy, Gentleman*, 1759

For young parents, parenting is all about having kids. This makes a lot of sense, because when you're young you can't fathom how anything can turn your entire world inside out and upside down like a pineapple upside down cake. Well, kids can do that. You have to feed them, change their diapers, sing to them, care for them, walk them, sit in ice baths with them to bring their temperatures down, wipe their poop stains from your shirt in the middle of meetings, calm them down in the middle of the night when all you want to do is sleep, and listen for hours and hours to people who have nothing but your happiness in mind tell you everything that you are doing wrong in parenting. Then there are those things that you should never do like throw a screaming baby out a window even if every fiber of your being is begging you to do it. Better to go out for a smoke or rob a convenience store. Maybe rob the store for smokes. Anything not to commit child abuse or murder.

But then, later on, you realize that having kids is just one part of parenting. Sure, it's an amazing part, a long part, an unforgettable part, but it's just one part. Another consists of having parents in whatever form that takes, whether actual parents in the traditional sense, a bevy of older cousins, a blended family, or all your friends down at Bob's Big Moose Tavern. By this I mean that kids, who are the future, have to be connected to your parents, who are the past. This is a circle that must be kept intact or else all kinds of misfortune can happen (see *sfortuna* in "Angelina in a Casket"). It's like this: just as you are forming that image of who and what your kids are, you also are being drawn back to an image of your parents, maybe slowly, imperceptibly, but it is happening. As an example, in the same way that I have an image of Lena, Rose, and Deanna at the back door of our house under the elm trees in San Jose, I have an image of my mother from a photo my father took of her sitting on a park bench on Staten Island in a winter coat with a fur collar and her hair swept up, her arms around me and my younger brother. Whenever I think of my mother, she is an Audrey Hepburn-looking twenty-something on that park bench in winter with lipstick and big brown eyes, which is probably where Deanna got them.

So, we are all working from a script, an archetype of father, mother, husband, wife, son, daughter, lover, poet, pirate, king, and everything else from Jung's *Book of Dreams*. The archetype of my mother from the bench has certain characteristics. Studying the photo, you can see that she is energetic, smart, teasing, sharp as cheddar, flirtatious, loyal, not patient with fools, and not kind to the dim-witted.

"Wow, you got all of that from one photo?" you may ask.

Well, yes and no. I am only able to see those things now, because I have been endowed with a new pair of eyes. It takes a while to get this vision, especially if you're focused on strollers, play dates, vaccinations, and trying to avoid the fact that, if the truth be known, you'd never have kids again even if they paid you with a lot of zeros and commas, as the Trace Adkins song goes (the Country singer, not the diet doctor). The "they" here is unclear, but in bitching it is a universally understood constant like the velocity of light in a vacuum (c), which I learned during my basement investigation of vacuum tubes is 299,792,458 meters per second or 670,605,749 miles per hour, which is pretty fast. Why it is forty-nine and not fifty is beyond me, although I accept it just as I once accepted the speed sign on a curve that said "19."

When it comes to universal constants, I am reminded of that particular moment during dates when I turn around and say in response to a pointed barb, "You know [insert name here], I don't remember the wedding." This comment, a barb in itself, is in the style of another universal constant that I have dubbed "the marguerite" in honor of my mother, whose name is Josephine but who had a sister named Margaret who died of tuberculosis at the tender age of twelve. The name was shortened to "Margie" under the influence of a popular song of the same name recorded in 1921 by Eddie Cantor and 1940 by Django Reinhardt. Then, because *margherita* means "daisy" in Italian and is the name of a political party as well as a style of pizza (tomato, sliced mozzarella, basil, extra-virgin olive oil), Margie became "Daisy," which I suppose is better than "Rita" or "Margarita," the drink of choice of college students and related to another song by Jimmy Buffet. As if that weren't enough, *margarita* means "pearl" in Latin. So, my aunt's name easily could have been Margaret, Margie, Marge, Rita, Daisy, or Pearl. "Peggy" was not an option, since that is more of an Irish variation than Italian, although my sister, Jolie, was almost named "Peggy Sue," my mother being a huge Buddy Holly fan, especially after the crash. I've also heard *margherita* used for sunflower. So, my aunt could have been called 'Sunny." You see how complicated this can get and why my mother limits the use of the marguerite to stopping people from asking "asinine questions." Of course, she believes all questions are asinine.

I've begun a collection of marguerites, not all of them pointed barbs, but neither are they lighthearted quips about people, the world, and life. For marguerites are not like *madeleines*, Marcel Proust's almond, sponge-cake cookies dipped into Aunt Léonie's tea and nibbled with dainty-like precision. Many of them are attack marguerites, reflecting the more bellicose society we live in today, which I find ironic since much of the political talk lately has been about one world, one race, one planet, one love, etc.[14] Yet, we can't seem to get along at all what with school bullying, mass shootings, guys who wipe their butts with their hands firing rocket propelled grenades, insane guerilla-types kidnapping schoolgirls, and more charging of light brigades in the Crimea. Maybe that's what happens when people are forced to deal with one another as technology makes the world smaller, faster, uniform, and a lot more familiar. But familiarity is even more overrated than truth, and the consequences of overestimating it more severe. In a hundred years we could all be extinct or illiterate from calling each other "dude." I'm not sure which is worse. In the meantime, I am collecting mom's sayings into a *Compendium of Marguerites* so that some semblance of reason and order might prevail. Please note that there is an element in these marguerites of, "Are you kidding me? Come on!"

Mom taught me that without sarcasm—the tearing of flesh—people will almost certainly take themselves too

---

[14] There was a naval patrol vessel named the *USS Marguerite* in service 1917-1919. I wonder if my grandfather saw it crossing the Atlantic. I don't know if the French Navy ever commissioned a ship called *Madeleine*. I would think not, since it would be like naming a football team, "The Detroit Dainties."

seriously as was evident in a recent conversation with a friend of mine, who chided me for not taking her seriously.

"Look, if we're not going to have a serious conversation about this, then let's just stop talking."

"All right," I said.

I stopped talking, which was hard to do, because not only was the conversation completely ridiculous, but I was having fun with it. According to my friend, a brouhaha began when she invited two compatriots from Albania to a birthday party she was throwing for a niece. These two women had been married to the same man at the same time while still living in Tirana, the capital of Albania. This was a cultural faux pas on a grand scale (the invitation, not the bigamy), since everyone in the immigrant community knew to keep these two hellcats apart. It just so happened, however, that because of the complexity of trying to figure out who was on the invite list, who was off, and who was on standby, my friend had created, as they used to say in the pre-Vatican II catechisms, the near occasion of sin. Everyone knew not to leave these two alone for fear that they would rip each other's hair out even though— now here's the absurd part—the husband in question had been killed by a runaway mule cart years earlier. Apparently, even the sons and daughters could not be in the same room or they would end up breaking furniture over each other's heads, which can get expensive after a while. So, my friend's dilemma was how to ask them over in shifts, with each calling beforehand to make sure the other one was not there. I thought of the scene in *The Godfather* when Michael tells Fredo not to visit their mother while he is at the house. To make my friend's plight easier and convey how I really felt about the situation, I suggested she tell the wives that they were dead to her.

"The whole thing was stupid," I told my mother afterward.

"You can't fix stupid," she said. "Don't even try."

And that, dear reader, is a marguerite: you can't fix stupid. It is a basic marguerite, but a marguerite nevertheless. The marguerite could be considered a form of Italian-American haiku, except that it doesn't have the traditional rhyme structure of three lines and seventeen syllables. Even so, it is pithier than haiku, because it can work its magic in fewer than seventeen syllables and, with its turn of phrase, be even deadlier. It is more like a biblical parable in that respect. Also, notice that I said "fewer." Let me state for the record that I admire those supermarket managers who courageously mark the quick check-out lanes as "Fewer than 15 items." They should be applauded and hailed as patriotic Americans preserving the Republic from the stain of ungrammatical expressions such as "Less than 15 items" or—good, God!—"between you and I!" I can barely bring myself to write that last line. It reminds me of the look of horror on Daniella's face at the sight of a green dog hanging unceremoniously out of a yellow tree.

There is so much ugliness in the world that we must do everything we can to bring harmony and beauty into our lives in whatever way possible. In the mouth of someone like my mother (hypothetically speaking, since no such person exists), the marguerite is sharper than a samurai sword, slicing and dicing its way through stupidities, political correctness, false insights, delusions, pretensions, fantasies, blind alleys, smokescreens, cheapness, shallowness, gossip, mistakes, blunders, faux pas, faux wallpaper, real wallpaper, paper assholes, ordinary assholes, holes in the ground, bags of dirt, bags of hammers, bullshit, horse shit, horse manure, calumny, deception, perjury, manipulation, and prestidigitation (legerdemain if you're French). If used correctly and with a modicum of grace, the marguerite can also cure warts and minor aches and pains. It is like cod liver oil that way, which is making a comeback ever since Hollywood types began popping pills of omega-3 fatty acids. If this keeps up, people will start wearing celluloid collars again. Please do not misconstrue this as investment advice; nothing could be further from my mind. See a professional before buying time shares in Kuala Lampur.

The *Compendium* contains a nearly complete list of mom's marguerites along with definitions, examples, and cross-references to other marguerites as well as *madeleines*. I included the latter only because you never know. And, as has already been established, I never know. When I was younger, I used to eat Fig Newtons by the pallet, not only because I love figs, dates, raisins, and all manner of dried fruit, but because I thought they would do for me what the sponge cake did for Proust, except rather than send me into a reverie of time past, they sent me into the bathroom. When you have irritable bowel, you can't keep loading up on figs or four-thousand page French novels, which are pretty much the same thing. Marguerites, considered as a whole, constitute a worldview and consciousness not unlike Yogi Berra's witticisms, which, I think everyone would agree, are in a category of their own. I certainly understand the observation that "Nobody goes there anymore; it's too crowded" just as I understand the marguerite, "When you walk past a monkey cage, you don't stand there and wait for them to sling shit at you." This is a good example of the marguerite's richness, complexity, and earthiness, which some might find offensive, but there are many layers to it, and one should refrain from hasty judgments.

As an example, just the other day I was walking down Fifth Avenue, minding my own business, as I am wont to do, when all of a sudden I was accosted by a Buddhist monk in saffron robes and sandals. He pressed a gold prayer card into my hand that looked like a shiny bookmark, slipped a beaded bracelet onto my wrist, and opened a notepad for me to sign with a prayer intention. He did all of this in just a few seconds. It was like panhandling kung fu. There were other signatures in the notepad, so I added my name to the list, which is something

I never do—sign things without knowing what for, but, hey, the guy was a monk. What could possibly go wrong? Then he showed me a photo of a temple they were building somewhere. It was red, two stories high, and sat in the middle of what looked like a Walmart parking lot. I wasn't sure about any of this, because the monk never said a word. I couldn't tell if it was because he couldn't speak English or had taken a vow of silence. I think it was the vow, because all he did was grunt and point to various things: the list, the prayer intention (peace), and the photo of the half-finished temple. Then came the monastic punchline: he wanted a donation. Fair enough. I pulled out some cash, which was amazing in itself, since I hardly ever carry cash. I figure what for? But New York is a tipping culture. People in the service industry generally don't make enough to get by, so they have to rely on tips. And do they ever. Even cabs post "suggested" tip rates up to thirty percent. If it costs me seven bucks just to open the door and sit down, I'm not giving the cabbie a thirty percent tip, I'm sorry. I say this even after having driven a cab one summer while I was in college studying the jussive subjunctive, but that's another story for another set of nine lives. I think we're up to three sets now, which makes twenty-seven lives in all.

So, the monk wanted twenty bucks. Actually, he didn't just want twenty bucks, he *demanded* twenty bucks. I had a twenty-dollar bill I was saving to pick up my laundry, and I didn't want to give it to him. Not only that, but I had given twenty dollars one other time to a panhandler, mainly because I mistook him for an off-duty security guard at the university where I teach and thought he was down on his luck. Then I realized it wasn't the guy at all. That's when I felt down on my luck. I wasn't going to make the same mistake again (see "But Can You Type?" n. 2). I also felt scammed, since if the monk had been upfront about what he wanted, I wouldn't have accepted the bookmark and bracelet to begin with. I even tried to give them back, but he wouldn't accept them. I gave him ten dollars and turned to leave, but he grabbed my arm and pointed to the list of names again, every one of which had "$20" checked next to it. I looked at the monk. The monk looked at me. Then he tapped the notepad as if to say, "fork it over."

Here's another thing: I don't like being played, especially by somebody in robes and sandals. So I said no. I said it again and again, but he kept tapping the notepad and looking at me. Finally, I tried taking the ten back so I could give him the twenty, but he pulled away. Then I yelled "No!' He backed away, bowed, bade me goodbye with a gesture of prayer as if to say up yours (I thought of the squirrel), and disappeared as fast as he had appeared. I was so upset I went to the Hebrew Studies section of the main library on Fifth Avenue to calm down. It was the same place I had gone thirty years earlier, and I felt just as violated. What made it worse was the thought that I hadn't gotten very far in all that time: from cubic zirconium to Zen pandemonium. This time, though, there was a different guard.

I didn't ask for this treatment by the monk, and, technically, I hadn't met the first condition of the marguerite, which was to pass by a monkey cage. Strolling down Fifth Avenue is not the same as standing there like a schmuck at the Bronx Zoo. However, what is clear is that the monkey cage is not a physical space but a metaphor for putting yourself in a vulnerable position. The vulnerable position I had put myself in was not rejecting the shiny gold card and bracelet right off the bat. In my defense, the monk archetype threw me. What could possibly go wrong with a holy man? Then, just like Stanley Cross, everything went wrong, mainly because I broke Rule Number One for living in the City-that-Never-Sleeps-Except-in-the-Bronx-Where-Everything-Closes-at-8:00-pm: Do Not Engage. It's like the Federation's prime directive of non-involvement when visiting other planets. In that regard, New York City is a very sophisticated, galactic culture (but we knew that). By violating the prime directive, I became entangled with a monk and, thereby, exposed myself to monkeys slinging shit at me. You might say I *set myself up*.

I am mixing metaphors and marguerites, so let me go for broke and throw in another (!), which sums things up quite nicely. In Italian, it goes like this: *Quando si sceglie di nuotare nella caca, non ci si deve poi lamentare per il cattivo odore,* which, roughly translated, is: "If you chose to swim in shit, don't complain about the stench." Well, you can (it's a free country), but who's going to take pity on you? It should be noted that shit appears as a major theme throughout these marguerites, probably because it is an excellent description of so much of life as in "shoveling shit against the tide," which is one of mom's favorites, having spent more than a few summers at Coney Island (see n. 2). In addition, we all know that the darker the shit, the sweeter the rose, which could also be a marguerite, except my mother never said it. She leaves the more or less pedantic ones to the pedants.

Here's another marguerite, one that works on many levels and has a long history behind it even though, technically, it wasn't coined until recently:

"There are so many assholes around here, it's a wonder people don't wear their underwear on their heads!"

This reflects a certain antagonistic and distrustful attitude toward life focused on the less noble side of humanity. That's mom. I think it comes from her having had scarlet fever as a kid and spending months in public hospitals with overbearing nurses who weren't concerned about scrawny kids and their feelings, especially when there were young doctors with wavy hair and plenty of time to spare in close quarters during air raids (not that the Germans ever bombed New York, but there were plenty of drills, in a manner of speaking). Later, she had to sink or swim, literally, at summer camps for recovering kids in Upstate New York. Little Josephine had to toughen up quick or be chewed up and spit out by the long-limbed, black girls from Jamaica Queens who accepted her because she was Sicilian and darker than the other white girls, of which there weren't many. Those girls usually went to private hospitals. You add a Sicilian, fatalistic genetic structure, along with marriage to my father, the "Prince of Rosebank," and you've got all the makings for a short story entitled "Mamma Mia." Speaking of genetic structure, mom was cloned in subsequent generations in me (referred to as "Razor Lips" while growing up), my three daughters, and Daniella, who inherited the Sicilian dagger tongue and scrappy toughness, which she uses to full advantage on the basketball court. I've seen her spin circles around defending point guards as if they were the concrete stanchions I ran over with the Penske truck.

This Sicilian toughness (seriously, have you watched any episodes of *Commissario Montalbano*?), tempered by a New York attitude and sickly childhood, created the woman my mother is today. And yesterday and the day before that. This is perhaps best exemplified in a vignette that I have lovingly and logically entitled (Eduardo of Scouting fame would be proud):

The Shop Rite Don and the Salad Bar

Luca Torrella was the produce manager in the Shop Rite supermarket in the Northern New Jersey town my parents moved to after the four of us were out of the house. My parents are the only people I know who retired and moved to New Jersey. So, mom had gotten a job at the salad bar in the deli section of the store, which doesn't exactly constitute retirement, but I think she was retiring from home (maybe the prospect of living in a house by herself with my father). That meant that "Lucky," as his friends and family called him, was her supervisor. I discovered years later that a certain gentleman in a

Brioni suit and wearing a pinky ring (not from Zales at the mall) would come in occasionally and ask to speak with "Lucky the Pro." While waiting, Mr. Brioni would sniff the bell peppers, look through the broccoli, and tap the squash with his Mount Blanc rollerball pen. One time, "the Don," as mom called him, came over to the salad bar and wanted to know who was responsible for the "set up."

"What set up?"

"All this," he said, spreading his arms.

"I am."

"You are?"

"That's right."

"Nobody else?"

"You see anybody else?"

"No."

"All right, then. I get in at five in the morning and have everything ready by nine when we open. Why do you want to know?"

"It's amazing, that's why."

"What's so amazing about it?"

To be honest, mom was being modest. To be accurate, she was biding her time so she could size up the Don and his intentions. Nevertheless, if you have never been to a Shop Rite salad bar, you must scrounge up the bridge toll and drive there right now. It is an experience not to be missed and mandatory for every vegetarian's bucket list. Generally, the salad bars are expansive places made of tile, chrome, and squeaky clean, glass counters. They are filled with an assortment of ready-to-eat salads sitting in bins of newly-crushed ice that run the gamut from five or six versions of the standard chicken, tuna, potato, and macaroni to the more exotic Tuscan bean, lox, whitefish, shrimp, calamari, baccalà, Tabouli, Waldorf, and Babaganoush. There are also what I would call intermediary salads like cucumber and onion, antipasto, Caesar, Greek, Cobb, corn, carrot-raisin, celery, beet, polenta, spinach, and fruit. You can get seven or eight varieties of fruit, depending on the season and whether there was a drought in Southern California or an earthquake in Chile. That's not counting specialty salads like New England Chicken, Cajun Seafood, Dutch Potato, cranberry-almond-quinoa, and Cole slaw (sweet, chopped, shredded, or with oil and vinegar). Then there is an infinite number of non-salad side dishes like pickles, tomatoes, beans, nuts, dried fruit, olives from around the Mediterranean, broccoli rabe, pecorino cheese, and soppresata. My head is reeling from this veritable American Salad Book of no less merit and worth than the American Song Book I listen to on the radio every Sunday afternoon. My God, if I have to hear one more of those whining anthems by Stephen Sondheim, I will take a nosedive in my endive. But I digress.

"I-I-It's fantastic," the Don stuttered, shaking his well-coiffed head.

"I don't see what you keep going on about. I do this every morning."

"Really?"

"No, I'm lying."

"I believe you. It's just that it's hard to find that kind of work ethic nowadays."

"Sure, I work hard," mom said. "I've raised four kids, so I guess I know something about hard work."

"I guess you do."

"So, what do you do?"

"You don't know who I am?" the Don asked.

"No, should I?"

"I don't know, should you?"

"What is this, twenty questions?"

"What do you think?"

"I think that if you don't want a salad, I have other things to do."

"All right, give me a salad."

Mom stared at him. I don't blame her. I am reminded of the Russell Baker story about the guy who goes to The Six Borgias for an executive lunch and orders "a martini."[15] It throws the wait staff into chaos. Or the time Lena asked for "salami" at a deli on Arthur Avenue that had about a dozen varieties.

"You'll have to be more specific," mom said.

"Well, what's your favorite?"

"That depends. Sometimes I like simple and go for the potato with black olives and eggs, usually with onions; other times I want the goat cheese, Romaine lettuce, cranberries, and sliced pecan salad."

"I can't have goat cheese. It clogs my heart."

"Listen, if goat cheese is the only thing clogging your heart, consider yourself lucky," mom said.

"Got anything with pineapple? I like pineapple."

"How about pineapple chunks, pear slices, and Chilean grapes over cottage cheese?"

"I can't eat cottage cheese."

"The heart again?"

"No, the throat. Can't keep those little curd things down."

"Ambrosia?"

"No, thank God, not yet. I still have a good memory."

"It's a salad."

"Are you joking?"

---

[15] See "The Martini Scandal" in Barnaby Conrad, *The Martini: An Illustrated History of an American Classic* (San Francisco: Chronicle Books, 1995), 69-71.

"No, I don't joke about salad at the salad bar," mom said. "It's made with Mandarin oranges, coconut, marshmallows, and cream."

"What kind of cream?"

"Whipped or sour. We have both."

He thought for a moment and said, "Have you ever wondered why 'mallow' is spelled with an 'a' but pronounced like an 'e'?"

"Not really. But whatever your job is, I want it."

"Why is that?"

"So I can spend my time thinking about a's and e's instead of p's and q's."

"Hey, that's good, that's very good. But, tell me, do you do a lot of that here?"

"A lot of what?"

"Minding your p's and q's."

"Only when I'm working."

The Don paused, folding his hands together, and the pinky ring caught her eye. She didn't let on, which must have required a herculean effort. I've seen her make a fist and then bite it trying to hold her tongue.

"What do you know about Luca?" the Don asked. "I mean, is he a good guy? He must be to make sure the salad bar is so well stocked."

"Whatever the salad bar looks like is my responsibility, good or bad," mom said. "And as far as Lucky goes, I've got nothing to say other than we all have problems. He does the best he can, I'm sure. Of course, the man is a moron, but that's between him and God."

"I see."

"So what'll it be?"

"Ambrosia, I guess."

"Whipped or sour?"

"Might as well stick with whipped. You've put me in the mood."

The funny thing is that the Don was a board member of Shop Rite who happened to live in the neighborhood and would stop by every once in a while for a surprise inspection. He'd do things like poke the produce, squeeze loaves of bread, check that the floors were spotless, and so on. He had it out for Lucky, who had a reputation for sloppy management and harassing the Dominican girls who worked under him (again, in a manner of speaking). The Don had come in that morning, his mind made up to have Lucky fired, which he would have done if not for mom. Instead, he was given a warning, put into a retraining program, and eventually given a raise. I know all of this, because the store manager told Lucky, who confessed everything to mom. Mom told the rest of us after she left the store and moved to Las Vegas, where they have even bigger salad bars. Lucky sends her birthday cards to this day. I don't know whether she likes getting them or not, because, as she puts it, "The man was a great big slob with a sexual appetite bigger than his plate" (another marguerite). Either way, I suspect it's like getting a birthday card from your dentist. It is a reminder of someone you've been intimate with—certain intimacy being forced upon us—who in the end fades away and you barely remember. But isn't paradox what life is all about?

"Yeah, no shit, Sherlock," dad adds, having the last word.

www.ingramcontent.com/pod-product-compliance
Lightning Source LLC
Chambersburg PA
CBHW061433040426
42450CB00007B/1025